THE REAL

Jason
ROBINSON

BY HIS 'RIGHT-HAND MAN' DAVE SWANTON

EMPIRE
PUBLICATIONS

First published in 2005

EMPIRE PUBLICATIONS
1 Newton Street, Manchester M1 1HW
copyright Dave Swanton 2005

ISBN 1 901 746 48 8

Photographs courtesy of Clint Hughes, Simon Wilkinson, Sue Corden, Andrew Varley, *Sale and Altrincham Messenger* and the author.
Cover design and layout: Ashley Shaw
Edited by Stuart Fish and Ashley Shaw
Typeset in Berthold and Bembo

Printed in Great Britain by Antony Rowe Ltd., Chippenham, Wilts.

To Carole, thanks for everything...

CONTENTS

FOREWORD

by Neil Barker

Manchester Evening News

DAVE Swanton and Jason Robinson are a champion double act – both have successfully crossed codes and made their mark on and off the rugby field.

Swanny has to be saluted for having a major influence on Jason's glittering career. He is up there alongside Eric Hawley, John Monie and 'Inga the Winger' for having helped nurture the immense talent of one of the most naturally gifted sportsmen this country has ever produced. Swanny isn't a coach or a team-mate, but a man to whom Robinson owes a debt for the way he has helped with his profile promotion by telling the real story of this most private of men.

Swanny and myself go back along way. We both still had a good head of hair when our paths first crossed at Wigan Athletic's former Springfield Park ground.

I can say I soon became one of Swanny's 'pals' – I soon noticed nothing was ever too much trouble for a man who clearly had a good inside knowledge of how the media worked.

When he left Wigan, members of the local press corps were, to quote Al Jolson, "missing their very own dear old Swanny".

Their loss was another media outlet's timely gain – I have never known Swanny pass up the chance of a picture opportunity if this meant promoting either a club, player or a worthwhile appeal.

Invariably, it would be Swanny instigating the original idea.

He is innovative, creative and infectiously ingenious in this work and most amenable.

Clubs have tried to replace him but have failed miserably. Those coming in hoping to fill his much-travelled boots have failed and couldn't hold a candle to this master of media promotion.

One quick telephone call whatever time of day is normally all it takes for Swanny to trigger a storyline and conjure up a back page like only he can do.

This is a man they say can sell sand to the Arabs – he's the original champion spin-doctor with the copyright on all the best prescriptions!

Swanny's style is not to lead a reporter up the garden path, he will never duck intrusive, hard-hitting calls and then serve up a cock and bull story to cover his tracks.

This fellow always calls it how he sees it. What a pity more clubs don't have Media Managers who are on the same wave-length.

Dave may not be everyone's cup of tea, but in my view he immediately falls under the put the kettle on, brew up, two sugars please and pass the biscuit tin category. He is worth his weight in gold when it comes to meeting the demands of the modern-day hack.

I can honestly say to you, Swanny, it's a pleasure knowing and working with you and thanks for all those back page leads!

I've lost count of the number of times you've got the sports editors off my back by delivering the kind of story only you have the balls, knowhow and ability to offer.

Neil Barker
Wigan, July 2005

THANK YOU

I would like to thank Carole, my wife for backing me in writing this book, for helping me with my grammar, for all the tea and coffee she provided me with while I spent months writing the book, but most importantly for being Carole, my wife, my best friend and for helping me to where I am today.

To my son Dan, who worked for two years at Sale Sharks and for giving me plenty to write about and share with you all.

Thank you, to Emma, Carole's daughter, for helping me in my early years in media.

My Dad, Fred, who took me all over in my youth watching all types of sport and my late Mum Christine for always being there when I needed her. Grandad Swanton who died in 1989, but helped with my introduction to sport all those years ago.

To Brian Kennedy and Ian Blackhurst who let me share their dream back in 2000 by inviting me to join them at Sale Sharks and for their guidance, backing and friendship.

Quentin Smith, the Sale Sharks Chairman who is a lovely man with a brilliant legal brain who has been a good friend for the last five years.

Chief Executive Niels de Vos who joined the club in 2002 and has taken the club to the brink of greatness, which will happen in the near future. He is also the best wordsmith I have ever known.

Kevan Taylor, the former Finance Director at Sale Sharks, for his friendship and guidance and for showing me how to work one hundred hours a week! To my old mate Mick Hannon at Wigan Rugby League Club, who I met in 1998 and has remained a friend and sounding board over the years.

John Monie, the Master, who took me under his wing in 1998 and taught me so much in a very short space of time at Wigan. John is a great coach, lovely man, and a very shrewd operator.

My good friend Mike Latham who I have known for nearly ten years and is always there for a chat about Rugby League; he hates Rugby Union, but I'll forgive him for that!

Colin Dawber who I have known over forty years since I lived opposite him on a council estate in Leyland. Colin was 'Mr Leyland Motors Football Club' and allowed me to travel with the team all over the North and, more importantly, taught me all I know about dealing with players. Colin has stuck with me through thick and thin and never fails to re-mind me how bad I was at playing cricket!

My great friend John Fillingham at Wigan Athletic who gave me my first job in professional sport twenty years ago and rescued me from the greenhouse in 1996 by taking me on at Warrington, then moving me to Wigan in 1998 where I met Robbo. Filly is a great Commercial and Marketing Manager. I enjoyed every minute working with him.

John Martin of Wigan Rugby League Club, the best Chairman the club has never had.

Peter Norbury, Phil Clarke, Mary Sharkey, Keith Mills and Mandy Johnson at Wigan, for their friendship and loy-alty when I worked at the club.

John Oakes, and his son Phil at Micron Video in Wigan, who gave me a start as a rugby commentator, are still good friends.

Henry Morris who is a great servant to Rugby League and big Wigan fan. His bakery also makes the best vanilla slices that Jason and I have ever eaten!

To Laura Bogard, Sian Masterton and Clifford Bloxham at Octagon for looking after Robbo so well and for your friendship.

Mike Workman of Puma who is a top man and looks after Robbo so well.

Jim Mallinder and Steve Diamond, the former coaches of Sale Sharks. Both have moved on to other roles. At Sale Sharks they were an unlikely, but successful duo, and helped me so much.

Philippe, Kingsley, Mark and the backroom team at Sale Sharks who make my job easier. Club Doctors Dave Jones and Geraint Allen together with England Doctor Simon Kemp for patching up Robbo so he can perform on his grass stage.

Lisa Robinson who has been at the club since the day I walked in back in 2000. Lisa is the Merchandise Manager at the club and is brilliant at her job but won't give any more discount than she has to!

Geoff Green and John Everton who have acted as Press Officers at the club and make my job easier, not easy, during the season. John also a spent a week proofreading this book. I shared a room with John once at an away game but never to be repeated, he snores too much.

Paul Cullen, the Warrington coach, who introduced himself to me on my first day at Wilderspool in 1996. A fierce competitor in his playing days, Paul is quickly becoming a top coach.

The media in both codes of Rugby who I have had the pleasure of working with. Thanks for your column inches and coverage.

Angela Powers of Sky TV who helped me develop the 'Billy Whizz' character in Jason back in 1998 and Euan Kerr, the Editor of *The Beano* for helping us make it happen.

Vicky Gomersall and James Cooper of Sky TV, Mike Hall, Alastair Mann and Chris Hall of Granada, Howard Booth, Andy Buckley and Richard Askam of BBC Look North West, Mike Bradley of Channel M and Ron Roby of BBC GMR, who, have become friends of the club and are always there to help promote the Sharks.

My great friend and former boss Peter Deakin who sadly died in 2003. Deaks took me to Warrington in 1999 and introduced me to Brian Kennedy and Ian Blackhurst in July 2000. Deaks taught me so much in a very short space of time. I miss him terribly but give him regular name checks to keep his name alive. Deaks was an all round top man who is now a marketing guru in heaven.

To Richard Prescott of the RFU and his Communications team, for looking after Jason when he is away on England duty. Richard has become a good friend over the last five years and is well respected by Robbo.

To the staff at Sale Sharks and Anne Blakeney, Chairman of Sale Sharks Supporters Club who make going to work a pleasure.

I always wanted to write a book and have been waiting for the right moment and the time came earlier this year after a meeting with Stuart Fish of Empire Publications. I had floated the idea but nobody took me seriously, apart from Stuart, who is a big Sale Sharks supporter. Thanks pal, I appreciate everything you have done for me to make this happen.

To Neil Barker of the *Manchester Evening News* for writing the foreword. I call Neil 'Elliott Carver' [James Bond film character] as he writes tomorrow's news today. Neil has been a good friend for over twenty years who also listens to my BBC Radio Lancashire music show on a Saturday evening!

To John Clayton, the Managing Editor at BBC Radio Lancashire, for giving me a chance to present my weekly radio show back in 2001 and is a big Wigan Rugby League fan.

To all the players I have had the pleasure in working with at Warrington, Wigan and Sale Sharks, I must say a Big Thank You.

Finally to Robbo for providing me with plenty to write about, leaving me with memories that will stay with me forever. He has been a friend and companion for nearly nine years and I have enjoyed being your right hand man pal, it's an honour.

STATISTICAL CREDITS

Thanks go to Stuart Farmer Media Services for providing me Jason's Rugby Union stats and to Mike Latham who interrupted his ground hopping tour of the UK to provide me with Jason's Rugby League stats.

PHOTOGRAPHIC CREDITS

Clint Hughes who has been my club photographer at Sale Sharks for four seasons and is a great photographer and Mr Reliable.

Simon Wilkinson of SWPix, Sue Corden, the *Sale and Altrincham Messenger* and Andrew Varley for allowing me to use their photographs in the book. Finally, thanks to my brother-in-law, Alan Dickinson for burning hundreds of photographs on to CDs for me to be able to share with you.

INTRODUCTION

I saw my first game of Rugby Union at Preston Grasshoppers at the age of nine, but became more interested in the thirteen-a-side game of Rugby League after seeing Billy Boston play for Blackpool Borough in 1970. I followed Rugby League for many years, and was fortunate to get a freelance-reporting role for Preston Radio Station, Red Rose Radio, in 1983. I covered many sports, but was given the chance to cover the 'All-conquering' Wigan side in the late eighties and early nineties. I remember in 1992 covering a game Wigan were playing and a young man called Jason Robinson made his debut on the wing.

With the many personal problems I was encountering at that time, I drifted away from radio work, but destiny meant that the young winger Wigan had given a debut to, would play such a big part in my life for most of his career.

After getting divorced at the start of 1994, I went through a major transformation including seeing my Mother die after a long painful illness and having to bankrupt myself, before meeting my current wife Carole in October 1994, who I married eleven months later. I was working as a disc jockey in the evenings and working at a local market gardeners in Charnock Richard in Lancashire during the day.

During the early spring of 1996 I received a phone call from my good friend John Fillingham who invited me down to Wilderspool, the home of Warrington Rugby League Club. I had met 'Filly' at Wigan Athletic in the 1980s when I was a freelance radio presenter with Red Rose Radio. The role John had in mind for me at Warrington was that of match day presenter and Media Manager. The birth of Super League had coincided with a document called 'Framing For The Future' and one role that no clubs had in place was that of Media Manager.

My first game at Wilderspool was Warrington against St Helens, where the 'Wire' snatched defeat from the jaws of victory, literally. With five minutes to go Warrington led by five points and a break from St Helens centre Alan Hunte was terminated by a 'clothesline' tackle by Warrington full back Lee Penny. Penny was sent off and while regrouping Pickavance ran in a heart-breaking try which Bobbie Goulding converted.

I ran the Press Conference after the game and Filly was satisfied that I could fill the role on the cheap as Warrington never had the proverbial pot to pee in, and the local bailiffs were regular visitors to the offices during the week trying to obtain payment for creditors.

Filly and I worked hard with the pre-match entertainment planning and the media. I landed a role with Teamtalk to be the voice of Warrington on the premium rate telephone line. I had to submit a story a day to Teamtalk, which, with John Dorahy falling out with Iestyn Harris and Alex Murphy, as Director of Rugby was never a problem.

John and I pulled in favours galore to put on quality pre-match entertainment and we had White Plains, Bucks Fizz and Black Lace, to name but three heading up games at Wilderspool. Black Lace's rendition of *Having a Gang Bang* was amusing but I don't know about the appeal to the family audience!

Wigan were due at Wilderspool for the annual 'bloodletting' fixture mid-season and the game was played in the afternoon and shown on delayed transmission by Sky Sports. It was a painful afternoon for Jason Robinson because he was flattened by Paul Cullen. 'Cull' ran on to a sliced kick and took out Jason so early, that looking at it on television that evening the point of impact of Cull's tackle was made before the ball was on the screen! All hell let loose with Neil Cowie, Wigan's prop forward, leading the 'charge' on sorting out Paul. Poor Jason was flat out on the pitch and the game was halted for several minutes while he was revived.

The 'tackle' Paul made had an effect in that Robbo had a quiet game thereafter, by everyone's standards. I still joke with Paul about the tackle and he always says that the blame lay with the Warrington kicker, Iestyn Harris, who fluffed his kick! Paul has stayed a good friend over the years and I was delighted when the Warrington Board of Directors finally gave him the job as Head Coach after Darryl Van de Velde and Steve Anderson had left the club.

The season at Wilderspool drew to a close and all teams were adopting nicknames. Warrington had always been known as the 'Wire' but John Fillingham had convinced the Directors that the club needed a new image and Warrington were, from the end of 1996 known as Warrington Wolves.

The last home game of the season was against Oldham Bears and Warrington winger Richard Henare was on fire, scoring a hat trick before being head tackled. I was sat pitch side with Carole's daughter Emma, who was thirteen at the time. When Henare was in the land of the fairies captain Paul Cullen shouted to the dug out, "Doc, get Richard off, he is f**ked", to which Emma asked, "Dave, what's wrong with Richard's foot?" Thank goodness for the innocence of youth and that Emma had misheard Cull's instructions!

A week later, Warrington received a severe thrashing at St Helens and Saints were crowned champions after the game. This game was a sad landmark for Paul Cullen who played his last ever first team game for the club as his knees were buckling under the strain of summer rugby.

Sadly, John Fillingham left Wilderspool after a huge row

with Chief Executive John Smith who had queried everything John did. Then again Mr Smith queried everything,
anyone did. He offered me a role at the club but wanted me
to work for nothing! After a bankruptcy that was the last
thing I wanted or needed.

I worked at Warrington Wolves in 1997, being paid late
every month, and the season started badly with a thumping
at Bradford Bulls. After the game the Warrington Chairman
got together with Mr Smith and Mateaki Mafi, Martin
Dermott and Willie Swann were all sacked. On Good Friday
I was meant to travel to Sheffield Eagles with Warrington
but pulled out, as I had to have my faithful Labrador dog,
Sam, put to sleep. Warrington got a good hiding and the following day Coach John Dorahy was packing his belongings
after getting the sack.

Easter Monday 1997 was a great day for the Warrington
Wolves' club and supporters. Wigan were the visitors and
even without Henry Paul and Gary Connolly, Wigan looked
very strong to the point that the local bookies had shut their
doors when vast numbers of Warrington fans were backing
Wigan to win.

The game started, and within half an hour Warrington were
over twenty points up with Nigel Vagana having a fantastic
game. We used to play pieces of music after Warrington tries
and I had only taken one CD with me for the game. When
Kelly Shelford went over for Warrington I played *Tom Hark*
by the Piranhas (a hit in 1980). The supporters went wild.
The tune proved so popular that it is still used for tries scored
by Warrington eight years later. I tried to license the track
and an agent I knew contacted the copyright holder who
wanted very little for the rights. Mr Smith said he thought it
was a waste of money, enough said! It is now played all over
the country at football, Rugby League and Rugby Union
grounds, including Twickenham. With hindsight, I should

have licensed it myself but thought it was a great commercial opportunity missed by the club.

During 1997 a new commercial radio station opened in Wigan called Wish FM and Head of Sport, Frazer Dainton (now with Sky Sports) gave me some freelance work covering games at Central Park, Wigan on Friday evenings, which I was able to do as Warrington played on Sunday afternoons. The job entailed covering Super League games and then interviewing players before returning to the studio in Orrell. After one of my first games, I had to approach Jason for an interview and he was very obliging and enthusiastic. I used a mini-disk, which fascinated Jason when he asked to hear the interview afterwards and could not believe such a small machine had replaced the massive tape recorders that were usually used. After one interview he said to me he didn't like a question I had asked and the answer he had given and that he would like it erased. This was to be my first real introduction to the professionalism and attention to detail Jason expected. The 1997 season rounded off with Wigan winning the Championship at Old Trafford. Warrington had lost at Sheffield in the play offs and Mr Smith was worried how the club would pay its bills during the winter months ahead, I pointed out that the sales from *Tom Hark* CDs might have helped!

I was still being paid late or not at all, and it was causing friction at home with Carole. I was working during the day at Blackburn College, teaching media as well as several residencies as a DJ, but at one stage Warrington owed me three months money.

In December 1997 I received a call from John Fillingham who was now Commercial Manager at Wigan following Dave Whelan's take over. John asked me to work as presenter at Central Park on Boxing Day in the Wigan v St Helens game. John also said that there might be an opportunity for a position for me as Media Manager in the coming months. I did the job as presenter and waited for the call to leave Warrington to join Wigan.

1998 started off with Warrington and the club had signed Adam Fogerty who had previously played at St Helens. Adam was also moonlighting as a movie star and featured in the film *Up and Under*, based on John Godber's play. I decided the only way to get the Warrington Wolves into the news was to use Adam's off-field role to get column inches for the club. Adam enjoyed every moment of his media attention and was a pleasure to work with. Warrington were drawn at Wakefield Trinity in the fourth round of the Challenge Cup and won easily. This prompted the Warrington directors to take up religion and pray for a 'money-spinning' fifth round tie. Mr Smith sat us all down in the office and delegated all the jobs for the new season. Then he told us he was going away on holiday just as we approached the start of the season and the fifth round tie at St Helens, although he would be back on the day of the game! He was more interested in Warrington's head of security organising stewards to stand at turnstiles at St Helens with hand held clickers to make sure that the Saints told the truth on the gate figure! St Helens won a spiteful game shown live on BBC. Warrington's tactics had wound up St Helens coach Shaun McRae so much that McRae lost his cool and had a real go at Warrington in the post-match interview shown live on Grandstand. I had sat through the game with Carole and her daughter Emma and my son Dan, hoping and praying Wigan would call me.

Three days later, the call came from John who wanted me to go to Central Park to meet new Chief Executive Phil Clarke. Phil was late for the meeting, but after our brief meeting promised me the job as Media Manager. I started at the St Helens game in the Challenge Cup quarter-final. Over 17,000 packed into Central Park and due to the usual

Match Day Presenter's unavailability, I had to fill in.

The game saw Wigan beat St Helens thanks mainly to a length of the field run by Jason Robinson who was given the ball by Danny Moore ten metres from the Wigan line before racing the full length of the pitch to score. The try, shown live on television was perfectly described by commentator Jon Champion as "A race only one man could win." I will also remember the game for a tackle by Andy Farrell on Chris Joynt, which was awesome. Faz hit Joynt across the chest with one of his massive arms and Joynt was on his knees gasping for breath. Denis Betts had returned to Wigan and came on as a second half substitute to score a great try. The day after the game, Wigan held a high profile media conference to introduce Wendell Sailor as a new signing. As you are no doubt aware, the signing did not actually happen and I was so glad that Wigan had screwed this up without my input, as the small amount of credibility I had built up would have been in shreds!

The problem Wigan had was that Kevin Ashcroft was in post as Media Manager and I had to work like a Ninja with powers of invisibility! The following week, Kevin was relieved of his post and I was genuinely upset for him as Kevin was and still is, a good friend. Wigan could be ruthless in matters like this and I realised that I needed to be very good as Media Manager to avoid following Kevin down the road.

My role at Wigan was part-time Media Manager working three days a week and game day. In your dreams! Wigan was and always will be a full-time role. I was also still working at Blackburn College and it was hard work combining those jobs with work as a DJ in the evenings.

On the day I arrived at Wigan to start work, John Fillingham met me and showed me to my office, which was in a back room of a terraced house in Hilton Street, adjacent to the ground. A desk with three legs and a chair with a broken back was my inheritance. A diary lay in the drawer, covered in dust but in good condition for a book eight years old! The office was damp and I spent the first few hours throwing all the rubbish out. Vice-chairman John Martin paid me a visit and said, "I have heard great things about you and what you are able to do for us, lets hope I heard right." Some people said that John Martin was not very pleasant but I dug in and thought I am going to get on with this bloke, which, thankfully, I did and still continue to do to this day. He is a great bloke and the best Chairman that Wigan Rugby League Club never had. John Fillingham said that if I worked hard and kept busy, John Martin would leave me alone. One thing that I have never shirked is hard work! John Martin said to me, "Go and see the kit manager and get some Wigan clothing as *I don't want to see you wearing Warrington clothing again.*" Great tip that for anyone who changes club in an administrative role, day one or maybe day two, wear your previous club's clothing and they always sort you out!

The phone rang about eleven o'clock and I was summoned to Chief Executive Phil Clarke's office. When I arrived, Phil had a form for me to complete to be paid monthly (what an improvement that was) and then told me that we were going to media train the players the following day. Dave Hadfield (*The Independent*) Mike Sudworth (Wish FM) and Bill Arthur (Sky Sports) were coming down to coach the best out of the players for future media work. I was told to report back to Phil on how things had gone. I thought to myself that I would be surrounded by some of the world's greatest players, and here is Phil asking me to criticise them. I thought long and hard that evening on how to play things and thankfully my plan not only worked, but I still use the plan today at Sale Sharks.

We split the players into groups and told them all that the media day was to help them to project themselves in the media, so as not to sound like sportsmen who freeze in front of the camera, microphone or journalist, and to remove the clichés of "take every game as it comes", "a game of two halves" etc.

We were also going to 'role play' talking to sponsors after a game and then all the groups went off to be media trained. My group were going to be interviewed by media as though they had won the 'Man of the Match' award (my work as a DJ came in useful, I can tell you).

First up was Rob Smyth and Rob was fine. After the interview he was applauded and wolf whistled by one man, Jason Robinson, who said, "I'm next!"

After seeing him make his debut six years earlier, floored by Paul Cullen, race the length of the field against St Helens and do a couple of Wish FM interviews, up he strode.

Robbo said, "It will be different from the radio interviews you have done in that it will go out live and we can't edit it, can we?"

"Blimey," I thought, "first Jason Robinson remembered me from my interviews and secondly he genuinely wants to get involved and wants guidance."

Jason was a star and after the media day stayed behind to not only thank me, but to tell me how much the boys needed a strong Media Manager, and could I help him with some of his fan mail. From that day in March 1998 I think I became personal assistant to one of the greatest players ever to play either code of rugby.

CENTRAL PARK ARRIVAL

I settled in pretty quickly at Central Park, mainly because the ground was only eight miles from home, rather than the sixty-mile round trip to Warrington.

I was given a key to the front door of the terraced house in Hilton Street and after a couple of days the girls in the front office moved upstairs and I took over the front room where I was able to see everything going on.

The second weekend into the job, was semi final weekend and Wigan were due to meet London Broncos at the McAlpine Stadium in Huddersfield. The Press Conferences at Warrington were attended by a few rugby writers but Wigan was different and as the players referred to it, "They are all over us like a cheap suit."

I closed all outer doors and set up a Press Conference area in the executive suite in the tunnel. The press were invited for 12.45pm and were given tea and biscuits and the players arrived by an internal door at 1pm prompt. John Monie, who I refer to as the 'Master' was very helpful with arrangements and we set up seventeen tables where the players would sit down to do 'one-to-one' interviews with the assembled press. Jason waved me over to his table and said, "Swanny (a nickname I have had for most of my life and soon picked up by the players), this is well organised but there are no milk chocolate biscuits on this table, we only have custard creams and rich tea." The press on Jason's table thought it hilarious but it was Jason's way of breaking the ice and getting the press loosened up.

John Monie was being interviewed by almost every journalist present and was the ultimate professional. Always smart, he also cast his eyes around the room to see that all the players were "behaving the Wigan way," as he termed it.

The players then had a team photograph taken and as these were pre-digital days you had to wait for the photographs to be developed before you could see the result. When printed, they clearly showed Denis Betts acting the goat as a hunchback, and the photos had to be taken again, which angered John Monie.

When the media day had finished, I sat with John, Jason and Neil Cowie while we finished off the warm tea and biscuits. Jason and Neil then opened up to me. Neil said he didn't trust the press, as he had been locked up in the local police station over a story about a proposed move to Leeds that he knew nothing about. Jason said that his past life as a 'bit of a hell raiser' seemed to be all the press wanted to talk about. But now things were different, Press Conferences were controlled and Neil, as unofficial shop steward, said the players thought I was a good lad, despite being bald and overweight! From Neil that was a compliment and we grew to respect one another during my time at the club.

Jason said, "Oh Swanny, I have something for you in the car, can you come and help me with it?" I followed Robbo on to the car park to his car and he handed me a carrier bag. "It's full of letters I told you about. I get them from fans and I am not very good at replying; can you help?" This meant could I reply to them all, and send an autographed picture to each of them. I told Robbo I needed to get some action pictures for him to sign. "Great, I will call into your office on Friday to sign them." Two days to organise this and over a hundred replies needed, I'd better get motoring. I pulled in a favour from a rugby photographer I knew and had the prints waiting when Jason called in to my office. He sat down and signed them all in his own hand and anyone who has a Jason Robinson signature will know that it's a work of art!

"Let me help you put them in envelopes," he said. I thought he was really good to offer this until he winked, produced another carrier bag and said, "These are some more letters I found in the boot of my car!" He also produced a second carrier bag and said, "I have brought you some of my old rugby clothing."

I was gob smacked and said, "Hang on pal, you don't want me to do your washing too, do you?"

Robbo just folded up laughing and said, "No it's Wigan and Great Britain 'stash' I have had at home and thought you might like it as a 'thank you' for helping me out."

He then wrote down his mobile phone number for me and asked for mine and said, as he was leaving, "Just one thing before I go Swanny, I don't like people swearing. There are far better words to use than four-letter ones." He was referring to a phone call I had received from Warrington while dealing with his autographs when they told me my final pay cheque was not going to be paid in full. I had hit the roof, and told Jason about it. He said the best way to deal with it was legally and by using the contacts I had in the game. Here was Jason Robinson, aged 24, offering me advice and really caring about Warrington not paying up! Over the years I have confided in Jason a lot and he has done the same with me. I can also say that day was the last time I ever swore in his earshot!

Wigan won the semi-final at Huddersfield with Jason scoring early in the game. Andy Farrell was inspirational in his leadership and Wigan were back at Wembley for the first time since 1995.

The players were back in training the day after for a briefing, and tickets for the final against Sheffield Eagles were put on sale. Wigan had suddenly come alive after five years in the wilderness. The queue for tickets started at the lottery office and went as far as the end of the car park. Robbo popped his head around the door and said, "It's great here when we're on a roll, I'm going into town, do you want anything from McDonalds?" Here is a supreme athlete eating fast food, I thought. "Go on then, I'll have a Burger and fries."

He replied, "That's a Big Mac and fries and do you want a doughnut to dunk in your strawberry milk shake?"

"Er, no thanks, just Big Mac and fries."

He arrived back ten minutes later, and said, "Close the blinds of your office, will you?"

I thought it was to stop the fans looking in but Robbo told me it was because the new conditioner Marty Hulme hated fast food! "I need fast food like this to keep up my energy levels," he said. I must point out at this stage that Jason always has been on strict diets set by his conditioners but is partial to fast food, and it never seems to affect his performance.

I thought if a star player like Robbo could shift fast food, it would be okay for me too! The number of times I have been to fast food outlets with Jason over the years makes me wonder how he is not built like the 'Nutty Professor'.

The 1998 Super League season started with a win over Castleford at Central Park, followed by a tremendous 38-18 win at St Helens on Good Friday. Robbo scored a great try and it was so well liked by Sky Television that they used the footage of his run to promote the television coverage for the rest of the season. Robbo joked that he would have liked payment for Sky using his image. I thought he was joking but years later I realised he had been serious.

I had to organise all the player appearances at Wigan and fill in sheets with dates, times, venue and directions and most of the players were as good as gold. Jason said he could not do anything after games played on Sunday, not even for sponsors. I thought it was something to do with his religion but he told me that together with some friends he went to 'Chinatown' in Manchester on a Sunday evening to help the homeless with food and clothing.

I asked him where he got his supplies from and he said donations from fans and people from his church. I did some ringing round for Jason and one Wigan sponsor, Henry Morris, who owns Morris's Bakery in nearby Coppull, was only too pleased to help. Henry has become a good friend over the years and when Jason's autobiography was published in 2003, Robbo asked me to send Henry a signed copy.

Jason didn't talk too much about his work in Moss Side but did tell a great story when he produced some clothing for a young teenager, only to be asked, "Have you no Adidas, Puma or Nike clothing mate? I can't go out in these!"

Team comedian Terry O'Connor suggested that Jason give some clothes to Australian winger Mark Bell who had not stopped moaning since he had arrived about the cold climate in the UK. Mark was of Aborigine descent and like many Aussies failed to spot the leg pulling.

Wigan will for me always be the place in Rugby League where they were so professional on and off the field. One example was in the run up to the cup final we were all measured for suits and on the day of the final everyone was given a carnation to wear. The team travelled down two days before the final and all the back-up and administration staff travelled down on the day of the game.

We arrived at the stadium an hour before kick off and after taking in the atmosphere we moved to our seats. Directly behind me was a young blonde lady with a little lad on her knee. The youngster was no more than two and had a cherry-and-white top on with 'ROBINSON' across the back. I thought it must be Jason's wife and young son Cameron.

I introduced myself to Amanda who was friendly and thanked me for looking after Jason 'at work'. Amanda and I still laugh about the way we both look after Jason and she is always telling me to take some time off to have a break from him!

Wigan were labelled pre-match favourites at odds that had never been, and never will be matched. I had a pound on Jason, Simon Haughton and Kris Radlinski to score the first try and at 100-1 I had a pound on Paul Broadbent of Sheffield for the first try.

The game started and it was Wigan who were under amazing pressure and if you ever watch a video of the game you will see Paul Broadbent rampaging for the line, only to be halted by Kris Radlinski ten metres out. From the play the ball Mark Aston popped up a kick, which Nick Pinkney caught and scored. Pinkney outjumped Jason, who had taken a knock a little earlier. I was upset we had gone behind but more annoyed that Kris Radlinski had stopped my 100-1 bet on Paul Broadbent! Weeks after the final I told Rads about my bet and we still have a laugh about it today.

Wigan lost the game 8-17 and we were all in shock. No way would Wigan lose to Sheffield but they had and after an 8/8 start to the season, the wheels had come off!

That night the Radisson Edwardian Hotel at Heathrow hosted the reception and this event was a real eye-opener. After the speeches, one of which was by owner Dave Whelan, the players literally went wild. It was a Wigan ritual after every cup final, although nobody had told me about it.

To start with the players start ripping one another's suits off, literally and when you think of the strength of these boys, it didn't take too long. John Monie disappeared to bed with a bottle of wine as he was fuming the team had lost and all hell was being created in the function room of the hotel. All drinks were five pounds each and it was no wonder because the cleaning up operation the following day would have needed a big team of workers.

I was a little nervous when I saw prop forward Tony Mestrov making his way towards me wearing only his boxer shorts, so Carole and I made a sharp exit. Jason and Amanda were occupying the settee in the foyer, so I asked if we could join them. "Of course you can, sit down." In the corner of my eye I saw one of the players, completely naked, being chased down the corridor by another holding a huge rubber plant. I didn't want to know what was going to happen if he caught up with him!

"Crazy, this lot, you are better off out of it," said Jason and the four of us talked for an hour before retiring. It wasn't that Robbo was a killjoy; he exercised a "do what you want, but don't involve me" approach. One of the backroom staff told me later that before he had turned to religion Jason was one of the lads. There are many tales about Robbo in his early days but I think in many cases, the truth was stretched a bit to make them sound better.

The following week Wigan travelled to Sheffield Eagles for a Super League game and won easily but the cup final defeat had hurt the players badly.

The next game was at Headingley and new Leeds Rhinos coach Graham Murray had drilled his team well enough to inflict Wigan's first league defeat of the season. Wigan then went on an eleven match unbeaten run but something was wrong: Jason Robinson could not seem to score a try. He had suffered a blow in the ribs at Hull but seven matches went by and although Robbo was making plenty of metres on the pitch, his early season scoring form had deserted him.

The winning run came to an end in a spiteful game at Central Park when Leeds won 15-8. The Rhinos came with a game plan and that was to put the Wigan hooker Robbie McCormack out of the game early. Ninety seconds to be precise before Adrian Morley flattened him. Mick Cassidy took his team's revenge on Morley with one of the worst high tackles ever seen and Wigan were beaten up badly by the time the final hooter sounded.

The following week Wigan travelled to Huddersfield and

Jason's try famine was finally over. The first thing he did when he scored was to look up to the sky and thank the man upstairs. Wigan then went five games unbeaten to end the season on top of the league.

The players were invited to the Fatty Arbuckle's restaurant on Robin Park the following week to take the Fatty's challenge. If you ate a starter, a huge steak and chips and swilled it down with an ice cream you got a tee shirt. John Monie said it would be good for the lads to chill out and the winner was Tony Mestrov, closely followed by Robbo and Simon Haughton.

The final game at Warrington should have carried an 18 certificate. It was awful and blood was being spilt all over the place. Warrington's season was over after this game but Wigan had the play-offs to look forward to. In the first few minutes Warrington raided down the left and full back Lee Penny touched down, but in the process, viciously elbowed Jason above the eye, splitting it wide open. Robbo came off and needed stitches and then returned with a headband on. In the second half Robbo made a dart through the middle and Steve McCurrie took Robbo out by the eyebrows, splitting him again. The game ended with Wigan winning 30-24 but the dressing room was like a war zone and the table in the middle of the room was like a butcher's slab. My job was to take the media's requested player and coach to the press conference. The media had selected Henry Paul, who had announced a day earlier that he was leaving to join Bradford Bulls. John Monie had other ideas, "Doc, get Jason ready to walk, you can stitch him after, get me his towel with plenty of blood on it too."

We went into the Press Conference and when the press saw the mess Jason was in, they gasped.

John Monie then started by saying, "Rugby League is a hard game but what went on out there was a disgrace. I expect referees to protect my players and look at this," as he pointed at Robbo leaking blood. We walked back to the dressing rooms and John Monie said he had done this for a reason. "We have lost to Leeds twice this season when Stuart Cummings was referee on both occasions, and he was in charge today. I don't want him to be in charge of the Grand Final if we qualify." It worked because Russell Smith was in charge at Old Trafford. As I said earlier, John Monie was the master and poor Jason, on this occasion, was used as an exhibit.

I left Robbo by the dressing room door asking if he was okay. He just replied, "I am 24, I have had worse and will no doubt get thumped again before I pack it all in. See you tomorrow Swanny, and don't forget it's your turn to buy the McDonald's!"

I couldn't believe it, here was a guy who had lost a bottle of blood making jokes before he went to get stitched up! Wigan beat Leeds in the qualifying semi-final at Central Park and the first Grand Final beckoned.

Before the final I had a PR stunt for Jason to get involved in. He was known as 'Billy Whizz' but no one had ever exploited it, so I rang Euan Kerr, the editor of *The Beano*, in Dundee for a chat. Euan said he would get his artist to draw up a cartoon of Jason playing rugby against the legendary 'Billy Whizz' to present to Jason. I then contacted Sky Sports reporter Angela Powers who is the best person I know for filming features. Angela travelled to Dundee and saw the cartoon being drawn, and finished. The short film ran on the weekly Rugby League magazine programme, The Super League Show'. Everyone now knows Robbo as 'Billy Whizz' but Angela Powers' great work made it happen.

The weather on the day of the Grand Final was awful. It rained all day and the final was never going to be a spectacle, or so we thought. Richie Blackmore scored the opening try and Wigan were not playing well, then three minutes before half time Kris Radlinski was tackled 20 metres out and Jason ran in to the dummy half position. Robbo picked up the ball, pinned his ears back and dodged the high tackle attempts of Leeds to dive in under the posts... what a try! Andy Farrell kicked the two points and Wigan, against the run of play it must be said, were 6-4 in the lead. During the half-time break I was sitting with Carole and Mick Hannon, the Wigan Academy Manager, and in front of us was little Cameron Robinson, Jason's son, with Amanda and her parents. One of the Leeds players' wives' asked, "Is your Daddy playing in the game?" Cameron replied, "Yes, he's just scored!" The look on the Leeds players' wives' faces was priceless and I thought young Cameron was a chip off the old block with his humour.

After the break Leeds' indiscipline got the better of them and Wigan won 10-4 to become the inaugural winners of the Grand Final. Jason was awarded the Harry Sunderland trophy as 'Man Of The Match' to become the first player ever to win the 'Man Of The Match' award in both a Cup Final and a Play-Off Final. Jason attended the press conference and was a true professional as he always is. On the way back to the dressing rooms I asked him how he had scored the try. "Well Swanny, I am not very big and knew they were going high and after that Warrington game the other week I didn't want cutting again so I kept ducking and running until I saw the posts."

The season finished with a dinner at Central Park and the Awards Ceremony. Robbo had finished the season with most clean breaks (40) and most metres made (3426) and as he remarked, "not bad for a lad from Hunslet."

The players then joined up with Great Britain for the Test Series against New Zealand. Great Britain lost the first two and drew the third, but even though he was running on empty, Robbo was named 'Man of The Series'.

At Christmas 1998 Greg Florimo arrived as the replacement for Henry Paul and moved into his home in Eccleston, near Chorley, when the thermometer registered minus three. I had a van I used to carry my disco gear about in and Carole drove it from Central Park to Greg's home with all the Florimo belongings in. Greg said he didn't have a big enough fridge so I rang Jason who had just returned from holiday. "Leave it with me, Swanny, I have a spare one," he said. We both went round that evening to deliver it to Greg's house and his wife was fascinated with England. She said, "The superstores you have here only sell frozen foods." We burst out laughing when we saw all the Iceland bags in the kitchen, "No," I said, "we have Tesco, Morrison's, Asda and Safeway all within ten minutes of here." Then again, if you had just flown around the planet for the first time, would you know where to shop? Anyway, the Florimos had two fridges and had a great time in their two years in the United Kingdom.

Wigan failed, in my mind, to capitalise on the Grand Final victory and as the year drew to a close, we were nine months away from leaving Central Park to move across town to the JJB Stadium.

One final Robbo gem from 1998 was when it was announced that the Rugby League was satisfied that Wigan was now under the salary cap. The same day, Taffy, the Wigan groundsman handed in his notice to move to Salford. Robbo said to the players, "See, that's been our problem all along. They were paying Taffy too much for cutting the grass. We can probably get five new players now and still be under the salary cap!"

1998 had started at Wilderspool not knowing when I was getting paid and had ended at Wigan as Media Manager to the Grand Final Winners and a barrel of laughs with Jason Robinson.

LEAVING CENTRAL PARK

The 1999 season began with a busy mailbag to answer. Remember that while the world was learning how to use e-mail, Wigan had no IT at all and it was word processors, electric typewriters or just a biro.

The first PR job of the year was to organise Robbo to speak to BBC's *Songs of Praise* on the terracing at Central Park about his Christian beliefs for a future programme. The day was dry but bitterly cold as Robbo was interviewed. He had a flimsy coat on and I was stood about five rows back, behind the camera, feeling very comfortable and warm in my bench coat. After the BBC had left we returned to my office and I boiled the kettle while Robbo thawed out in front of the gas fire. Tony Hannan of League Publications had travelled over to interview Jason and asked him the questions as he recovered from the cold. Tony is a good journalist but while covering the subject of Jason appearing on *Songs of Praise* he made a mistake. He asked Jason how he had celebrated Christmas, and Robbo went into overdrive about Christmas being over-commercialised and that Christ was not born on December 25th and that neither he nor his wife celebrated Christmas at all. Tony was very professional, listened intently and then moved on, but I was then aware why Robbo had not sent me a Christmas card after I had posted one to him!

The next PR exercise was not a pleasant one, in that young hooker Jon Clarke was appearing in court after being involved in a fracas on the night Wigan won the Grand Final. Jon was, and still is a lovely lad and comes from a good family. He was 18th man on Grand Final night and as a youngster, all that aggression he had built up in case he was needed on the bench had to come out somewhere and sadly, instead of probably going for a run or knocking sevens bells out of a kick bag in the gym, he had got involved with a punter in a night club. Club Chairman Peter Norbury, a top solicitor, did his best representing Jon but the Judge sent him to nearby Hindley Remand Centre for six months. We issued a press release and then Robbo got together with conditioner Marty Hulme and some of the other players to see what they could do. Brian Foley, who was a retired policeman and in charge of recruiting young players for the club made some calls and Wigan did some of their training sessions at Hindley to involve Jon while he was a guest of Her Majesty.

At the end of January I was shopping in Wigan with Carole and my mobile phone rang. It was Peter Deakin who had taken over as Chief Executive at Warrington and wanted me as part of his off field team. I politely declined as I wanted to get the experience of closing a ground and writing a book, both of which proved good grounding. Deaks said, "Okay, but I will leave the offer open for you."

The cup draw paired Wigan with Leeds, in the fourth round as a repeat of the Grand Final. Wigan got an unexpected boost when Leeds prop forward Barrie McDermott was sent off for flattening Simon Haughton. McDermott was unhappy about the decision and Leeds seemed to build in stature and with only twelve men they beat Wigan 28-18, although it must be said Wigan finished with twelve men after Andy Farrell was sin binned for dissent with only nine minutes left. Defeat hurt Wigan, but hurt Jason even more as he disliked losing at Headingley. Leeds is his home city and he always pulled out all the stops against them. I think the problem was that they had turned him down as a youngster when he really wanted to sign for them. In rugby terms it probably compares to Decca Records turning down The

Beatles in the sixties. Jason had been a ball boy at Headingley and told me that every time the ball came his way he raced for it so he could throw it to his hero Gary Schofield.

Wigan's 1999 Super League season started with a win over Hull at Central Park with Robbo scoring a try. The next game was back at Leeds and Chairman Peter Norbury insisted all the players were to wear their Super League winner's rings to remind them they were better than Leeds. It seemed to have an effect as Wigan won 26-12. Jason failed to score but his support play was excellent.

Tickets for the final game at Central Park went on sale the following week as the countdown to leaving the ground had started.

The squad was fewer in numbers than in previous years and this was having an effect on the club. They were beaten, firstly by St Helens at home on Good Friday, and then suffered successive defeats against Halifax and at home to Castleford. The Castleford defeat left Chairman Peter Norbury steaming and as I went to get John Monie for the Press Conference, he overtook me, nearly knocked the dressing room door off the hinges before getting all the players together for a roasting.

Relations between Peter Norbury and John Monie had been strained for a while and this game was the beginning of the end for John's second spell at the club.

On Bank Holiday Monday Wigan won at Salford but we were so short of troops that Jason was switched to full back and rookie youngsters Liam Bretherton and Wes Davies (grandson of Billy Boston) were given a game and both scored. Robbo was outstanding at full back, scoring a hat-trick.

The following game, Gateshead Thunder visited Central Park and Wigan won 16-13. Not a classic game but Jason scored what I term as the luckiest try of his career. He ran on to a loose pass that had gone to ground, flicked it up with his toe, caught it, and ran sixty metres to score. Gateshead Coach Shaun McRae was a big fan of Jason and said, "You can't mark the guy at the best of times, but how do you coach against a try like that?" After the players had dressed I saw Robbo and said, "How lucky was that?" Like Christmas, I soon learnt that 'luck' is not a word in the Robinson vocabulary. "There is no such thing as luck, you just make the best of the opportunities you get, and by the way, I planned that," he said with a smile.

I think that was the first and only time I ever heard Jason lie! Now between you and I, if you ever get chance to watch that try, get in touch and tell me if you thought he had planned the move!

The season was moving on at a pace but seemed to be going nowhere. It was as though everyone was waiting for the doors to close at Central Park. John Monie confided in me that things were not well between him and the club and his cause was not helped with a 19-2 defeat at Bradford. Andy Farrell had been struggling with an ankle injury for a couple of weeks but when he booted over a penalty he was in agony. It was later diagnosed that he had broken a bone in his ankle and had played for three matches with the injury.

On the Monday morning I had to drive John Monie to Manchester to guest on the BBC's new *Super League Show* and he told me that he thought his days were numbered at the club.

Wins followed against London, Sheffield and Hull but the defeat at home to Leeds was the end for John and he was fired three days later. He came into my office in Hilton Street, put his arm around me, told me to look after myself and that I should carry on looking after Robbo off the field.

Robbo came in after lunch and over the years I have learned that he keeps his own counsel on important things, but I could see he was not a happy man. After a few minutes of reflection he said, "It's a cruel game at times but it is only a game."

We had to go to a local school the following week to show the children the Super League trophy and on the way back Robbo opened the glove box on the car and spotted my Drifters CD. "Oh great, I like them, take your time going back to the ground, then I can have a listen." Not only did he listen, he seemed to know all the lyrics and when he finally got out of the car he did a few dance steps too! A couple of years later, after making his debut for England at Rugby Union, he performed *Saturday Night At The Movies* on the team coach - every England debutant has to give the rest of the team a song.

Super League Europe, based in Leeds, had an idea to boost support in Scotland by taking the Gateshead Thunder v Wigan game on the road to play it at Heart of Midlothian Football Ground. If that wasn't a bad enough idea, they wanted me to take Jason Robinson and Denis Betts up for the day for a photo shoot. Now let me tell you that if you take sportsmen on a PR stunt, you have to do everything - plan the route, buy the train tickets, pick them up and feed them!

We caught the train at Wigan at 7am and sat back for the three-hour journey to Edinburgh. Denis, who is now on the Wigan coaching staff, was a Wigan legend and was easy to get a long with, but I was surprised at how little Jason knew about Denis and how little Denis knew about Jason. We arrived at the station and caught a taxi to Hearts' ground to meet Kerod Walters and Willie Peters of Gateshead, Ian Riddoch of Super League Europe, Mick Hogan, my opposite number at Gateshead and Captain Thunder (the Gateshead mascot who was themed on a superhero dressed in purple!).

Denis did some stunts with a football as he had nearly chosen a career in football before signing for Wigan and the boys did some interviews for the local media. Ian Riddoch had told me lunch was provided, but little did we know it was to be a sandwich, stood on the path in the street. Denis was fuming and Jason was not too happy either. The neighbouring streets around Hearts ground are similar to the set of the film Trainspotting and when one young, foul-mouthed jock hurled a tin of fizzy drink at the head of Captain Thunder we decided to move on and do the second half of the PR exercise at Edinburgh Castle. Great planning by Riddoch as it was the week of the Edinburgh Tattoo and the place was packed.

Jason's mother is Scottish and Willie Peters, although Australian, was of Scottish descent so the idea was to have the players in club jerseys and kilts! The changing room had not been planned for so Jason and Willie got changed in a turret and left their clothes on a cannon. While the photos were being taken my eyes drifted to Captain Thunder who was posing for photographs with some Japanese tourists. The little guard in all his customary attire was not happy. Now when Scottish people talk quickly it sounds as though they are picking a fight, have you ever noticed? The guard was gesticulating and waving his rifle in our direction and I caught the words "leave now." The boys were in stitches laughing and when the guard slowed down to how you and I speak he said, "You are not dressed in the appropriate manner for this castle." Robbo in a kilt with Willie Peters was a picture that I had to share with you in this book.

We arrived back in Wigan at 6pm and after dropping Denis off I took Robbo home. On the train they give you unlimited tea, coffee and biscuits and unbeknown to Jason, Denis and I had put about twenty packets in our pockets to stack in Robbo's dressing room pigeonhole the following day. Robbo always says that he threw them away but I doubt it!

Most of my time at Wigan was spent writing the final game programme and a book called *The Central Park Years*. I had a laugh with Jason years later when I told him that I had checked on eBay to see if they were worth anything and when I found them, I wished I hadn't as bidding had peaked at 99p!

The final day at Central Park was very special to everyone. 18,179 was the official crowd although it looked a lot more to me. Jason was not happy before the game as he had to spend nearly £250 on tickets for his family as all complimentary tickets, even for players, had been stopped.

Robbo had a great game setting up Denis Betts early on before scoring two tries of his own. It was a game Wigan dare not lose and was probably the most entertaining of the season. After the game, the players did a lap of honour and went back to the dressing rooms to reflect.

That evening, we returned to the ground for one last party and the person we all felt sorry for was Vice-chairman John Martin, who ran the Riverside Club at the ground. He treated us all to his rendition of Nessun Dorma, as he had a great voice.

The following day we started the move to the JJB Stadium before the bulldozers moved in. Tesco had bought the site and as Robbo said, "In years to come I can tell my kids I used to start my run at the deli counter, step in and out of the vegetables and then touch down near the televisions; better still, I will show them the video!"

The Wednesday after the final game saw the end of season awards at Headingley and I was fortunate enough to win the Best Media Man and Best Programme awards. Robbo found out the day after and came into the office to congratulate me. He also told the other lads and it was really special to get phone calls and visits from players like Kris Radlinski, Neil Cowie, Andy Farrell and Denis Betts, I can tell you.

The opening game at the JJB was a disaster as Wigan lost 10-14 to Team of the Year Castleford Tigers. The capacity was set at 15,000 and we attracted just over 13,000 to the game. Like the final game at Central Park there were no complimentary tickets for the players, which I could not understand as there was plenty of space.

All was about to change and the next twelve months were to become a rollercoaster ride. Firstly, Maurice Lindsay arrived back as Chairman and told me he had big plans for me and that he would review my wages. I was still on the same wages that I arrived on, even though that was based on a part-time position. I went on holiday with Carole, looking forward to working with Maurice, as I had always respected him.

The day I returned to work, I found out that Ian Riddoch had been appointed Marketing Director while I was on holiday. He started off on the wrong foot by saying, "Swanny, I am the boss so if you remember that, we will get along fine."

I was so annoyed; I picked up the phone and rang Robbo. He calmed me down and told me I was good at my job and he was sure other teams would want me if I wanted to move on - I had told him about Peter Deakin earlier in the year. Robbo also told me that the 2000 season might well be his last at Wigan as he fancied a move to Rugby Union.

I rang Peter Deakin and asked him if the job offer was still open from our chat ten months earlier and he said, "Of course it is and I will double what you are on at Wigan."

Taking out the swear words, I told Riddoch I was leaving at Christmas.

Let's just say the clash of personalities between Ian and myself had become unbearable. He was a Maurice Lindsay appointment, I wasn't, and I had to move.

My last game at Wigan was the annual Christmas money-spinner against arch rivals St Helens and several Sunday papers took a punt that 2000 would probably be Jason's last year in Rugby League before he moved to Rugby Union. I wonder where they got that from, I hear you ask? I cut the pieces out and blue tacked them to the notice board as I left after the game.

On the way out of the stadium, Neil Cowie came up to me, shook my hand and thanked me for everything I had done at the club for him and the players. I saw several others on the way to the car and I must admit I felt awful.

Little was I to know then, but my parting with Robbo would be brief.

FROM WILDERSPOOL TO SALE

Carole took me to Wilderspool to start work for Warrington Wolves as Wigan had taken my car back after the Boxing Day game. Peter Deakin met me at the door and had all his marketing team in early to welcome me. 'Deaks' was a legend in my mind and is so sadly missed by many following his death in 2003.

'All for one and one for all' was Deaks' way of doing things and my new work colleagues were Adam Jude (now in charge of Marketing at the Rugby League) and Steve Morris (now working for the National Hockey Association).

Adam was a local lad whose work ethic is second to none and we have tried more than once to get him to come and work at Sale Sharks. Steve was a former public schoolboy who was a very shrewd operator. Adam and myself speak with broad Northern accents and we used to rib Steve about how awfully posh his accent was.

First job at Warrington was to whip the media department into shape and I thought I needed to make a quick, positive hit. *The Sun* was running an appeal for readers to save crisp packets, as they could be exchanged for books for school children. I rang *The Sun* and got an early page story on the club.

Peter Deakin had worked some real magic by recruiting former Brisbane Broncos pairing Allan Langer and Andrew Gee along with Tawera Nikau, as the big names to draw the crowds. Lee Penny popped in to say hello and I must say I liked Lee but told him that the assault on Jason a couple of years earlier was disgraceful. He nodded and said it was something he was not proud of.

After three days in my new role my mobile phone rang and the voice at the other end said, "Dave Swanton, I hope you have not forgotten about me and the lads at Wigan." It was Robbo just checking up that I had settled in okay. We had a catch-up conversation and he filled me in with everything that had been going on at the JJB Stadium. Robbo finished by saying, "It's your turn to buy the McDonald's so I'll meet you at the Warrington branch one day next week." I still continued to deal with Robbo's fan mail from home, as Wigan had seemed to lose the plot in looking after the players' mail.

At the end of January 2000, Warrington travelled to France to play St Esteve in a pre-season warm up game. Peter Deakin invited me to accompany the team and we set off at 6am from Warrington on the coach to Stansted where we caught the plane to Carcassonne. Allan Langer could not believe the airline we were using. There was a tea and coffee machine at the front of the plane into which you inserted coins to get your chosen drink. Allan fell about laughing as the plane started reversing, getting ready for take off with people walking about in the aisles. The best was yet to come as we approached Carcassonne and the plane went right, then left, then right again before descending. Allan shouted, "I wish the pilot and his assistant would make up and decide who is in charge!"

The airport was something else too. No baggage collection point, you picked your own off the runway and made your way to Customs.

The coach driver was called Jules and he was a good bloke, apart from the fact he was drinking red wine from the neck of the bottle as he drove one handed on the winding road to Perpignan. About ten miles out my mobile rang and it was Robbo asking how the trip was going. "You would not believe it Robbo!" He said that it was better than the Wigan warm-up game that was at The Willows, the home of Salford, the following evening.

The hotel in Perpignan was in the town centre and was very comfortable. I got chance to have a chat in the bar with Peter Deakin, who wanted to run through some of the media ideas he had for the club. Deaks was an incredible man who came up with ideas and was the best 'networker' I have ever known. He knew so many people and introduced me to so many of them.

We won the game easily and the travelling Warrington fans had a great weekend. I must go on record by saying that supporters of Warrington are very special to me and they deserve a trophy to enjoy, and that under Paul Cullen that special day is not far away, I am sure.

Phil Oakes of Micron Video had travelled with us to film a diary of the tour – Deaks' idea – and we went out in the evenings to sample the local restaurants. Deaks' plan was to deliver a copy of the recording on video to Granada, Sky and the BBC to boost the Warrington Wolves brand and the profile when we returned. Suffice to say it worked a treat. We also sold 500 videos of the tour to supporters as a keepsake!

I stocked up with cigarettes and booze on the day we left and bought Carole some perfume from the big department store opposite the hotel. We flew home and on arriving back in Warrington the temperature registered minus eight. In the car on the way home I rang Carole and told her I was looking forward to some home cooking and I then rang Robbo to see how he had gone on at Salford. He said that Wigan had won and he had enjoyed playing alongside new signing Steve Renouf. I told him Warrington had looked good and he said, "When do we play you lot?" Quick as a flash I said, "Bank Holiday Monday at 11am, live on Sky." Robbo finished by saying, "Look forward to it and just for you, I'll score you a try!" "We'll see," was my reply.

The last few miles of the journey home were spent reflecting on the trip and the fact that I was enjoying working with Peter Deakin and how much I was learning from him.

The Super League season was launched at the Photographic Museum in Bradford and I drove over with Allan Langer's kit for the photo shoot. Allan drove over with coach Darryl Van de Velde but I preferred to go alone as Darryl was one of the most miserable people I have ever met.

After sorting out the changing area for Allan I went outside for a cigarette and walking towards me were Wigan Coach Frank Endacott, Captain Andy Farrell and Ian Riddoch.

Faz said, "Swanny, can I introduce you to Frank?" Frank, a true gentleman, said, "Pleased to meet you Dave, I have heard so much about you." I looked straight at Riddoch and felt 'ten foot high and bullet proof'. I never spoke to Riddoch, as although I was happy at Warrington I was still angry inside.

The fixtures I was looking forward to were those against Wigan Warriors at Wilderspool. The first was on May Day Bank Holiday with an 11am kick off. Carole and I stayed the night at the hotel opposite the ground and I was up bright and early for the game. I turned on my mobile phone and there were several messages from the Wigan players and one in particular from Jason saying he was going to score me a try! True to his word he did with an electrifying run from dummy half forty metres out. After the game I sorted out the Press Conference and made my way back to the tunnel to speak to Robbo. "Told you I would get a try for you," he said. "Thanks a lot pal, you could have tripped up or knocked on," was my reply.

Mid-season, things were happening behind the scenes with the new ground proposal for Warrington. A board of directors had been assembled and, having met them all, I agreed with the late Brian Clough's view of Chairmen and Directors. This lot did not have a clue and I was getting a little frustrated. At Wigan, Dave Whelan made all the decisions and we actioned them, here at Warrington it was a case of "a camel is a horse designed by a committee!"

Peter was talking to Brian Kennedy at Sale Sharks about a possible ground share with Warrington and he was involved in many meetings with Brian and his business partner at Sale Sharks, Ian Blackhurst.

Mid-July, Deaks took me into his office and said, "Swanny, we are going to Sale."

"Sail what?" I replied. Deaks laughed and whenever he did, his whole body joined in.

"No, Sale Sharks Rugby Union Club."

Deaks told me that we were moving over with a view to merging Warrington and Sale Sharks to play out of the new stadium. I told Deaks I was not keen on 'kick and clap,' which is a Rugby League term for Rugby Union, but Deaks said, "Look, I want you to ring up the owner Brian Kennedy and have a chat with him."

I did and must say it was the shortest interview I have ever had. Brian said, "Deaks has told me a lot about you and I know you are the man for me." I just listened and then Brian hit the right note by saying, "I want to build Sale Sharks into a top Rugby Union club and I believe you know one of my new signings."

"Apollo Perelini?" I asked.

"No, Jason Robinson is joining us at the end of the current Super League season and he thinks a lot about you too."

My mind was made up; it was a case of wanting to know the starting date, never mind the salary.

I rang Robbo that afternoon and said, "You kept that quiet about moving to Sale Sharks."

"I wanted to surprise you, and I told you that you couldn't

get away from me. My mailbags are bursting and I need your help. Why not come round with Carole to our house as I have something for you."

A week later I called round and Robbo produced a blue box and said, "Here you are pal, I won you a watch at Bradford Bulls." Robbo had been named 'Man of the Match' and he gave me his Tissot watch prize.

Jokingly I said, "I thought they would have given the award to Neil Cowie for that incredible drop goal!" Robbo laughed and said, "Don't ask Neil about the kick. He has been talking about it for the last week, saying that they are still looking for the ball on the main road outside the stadium!"

I had taken on the joint role with Mike Latham on BBC Radio Lancashire presenting League 2000 and I asked Robbo if he would be a studio guest. "Usual fee, a bag of chips on the way home?" he said.

Robbo did the interview so well and we had, over the previous two years, developed a way of distancing ourselves in interviews to sound as though I knew what I was talking about and he was so relaxed.

The last question I asked him, to put one over on him, was, "Where will you be playing your rugby next year?"

"On a grass pitch," was his reply. I read out the closing credits and once the news started fell about laughing.

In the car going home Robbo switched into serious mode and said, "Right Swanny, when I sign I need to hit the floor running, so can you get me some videos of Sale Sharks in action, and get a full set of photos, write down who the players are, how old they are, where they are from and what position they play. It's going to be tough after a full Rugby League season but if I can slot in with the players straight away life will be so much easier."

I took the photos round to Robbo's house along with the videos and left him to set about learning all about thirty-five new team-mates. I had the help of Geoff Green from the *Manchester Evening News* with the names on photos. 'Greeny' is a Sale stalwart and has covered the club from the Richard Trickey, Fran Cotton and Steve Smith days. Greeny is a man you can trust and he got the first interview with Jason when he changed codes in October 2000.

Robbo sat on his own in the stand at Heywood Road on game days watching the matches and studying all the moves. At the end of September, Deaks called me into his office in the portakabins we occupied at Sale Sharks, to tell me that he wanted my help. That was Deaks' way of delegating the job to you, but he was such a good bloke you always agreed. He said, "When Jason signs I want a big Press Conference with all the top journalists here, plus television, radio, you name it, get them all. I also want a video of Jason scoring tries in the way that only he can so ring Micron Video at Wigan and get help."

John Oakes of Micron had been a friend since my early days in Super League and could be trusted. Everyone knew Jason was moving to Rugby Union but no one knew where he was moving to and when it would happen. We used part of the 'Billy Whizz' video that Angela Powers had put together in 1998 plus some tries from his days at Wigan including one from the Middlesex Sevens, which Wigan had won in 1996.

Deaks was chuffed to bits with the video and said, "Right Swanny, the day Jason signs is Tuesday 17th October at 11am so get the place full and have a word with catering to sort out the buffet lunch." I think the lunch was for Deaks who loved his food!

Before the big day Jason had one more game to play for Wigan and that was against St Helens in the Super League Grand Final at Old Trafford. The night before the game, I rang Jason to wish him well and said I would be waiting in the tunnel after the game to "throw a media blanket over him." That meant he was talking to no one before his move to Sale Sharks. Jason was quite restless on the phone and I asked what the problem was. He said, "I can't believe Wigan, we have a big game tomorrow and I was not allowed to train with the team as I was wearing blades on my boots and they were afraid it would ruin the pitch at the JJB (blades are the alternative to studs)."

"Never mind," I said, "it will all change on Tuesday."

Sale Sharks were playing Caerphilly in the European Shield with an early kick-off on the day of the Grand Final. Sharks won the game in the rain in front of 1500 supporters.

I took Carole and Steve Hampson, a former Wigan legend and Sale Sharks' Assistant Conditioner in the car up the A56 and parked up at Old Trafford. I had offered to help the guys in the Media Department of Super League with an ulterior motive. Carole would sort out the programmes and press packs for the media and I would act as runner with a pitch side pass, which would get me into the tunnel at the end of the game.

Wigan went on to lose the final to rivals St Helens. Robbo had been forced to switch to full back as Gary Connolly was not fit and Kris Radlinski moved to centre. An hour before kick off Willie Peters was throwing up in the dressing room so Wigan were battling against the odds from the kick-off. I remember Robbo running through the middle and being brought down by Apollo Perelini, who was Jason's great friend and was also joining Sale Sharks. Later AP [Apollo] told me, "I gave him a little facial and told him we were not team-mates yet!" Apollo is a lovely man and always looked out for Jason, in fact in a game at Knowsley Road earlier in the season a fight had broken out around Jason and Robbo (all five feet eight inches of him) had decided to help break it up. The next thing you saw on the television was Robbo flying out of the melee, flung by Apollo who didn't want his 'mate' roughed up!

After the Grand Final I made my way pitchside and met Jason in the tunnel with Apollo and asked if they would be photographed together in their respective colours on the pitch (Deaks' idea) but neither were keen on the idea. One or two journalists asked for time with Jason and I said, "Sorry, he has played his last game for Wigan and will speak at the Press Conference at Heywood Road, Sale, next Tuesday at 11am, are you coming?"

I got called fit to burn but I was not ruining my big Press Conference for anything. After the journalists had gone Robbo said, "Thanks Swanny, it's like old times this, with you as Media Manager."

We said goodbye and arranged for Jason to come to Heywood Road on Monday for some photographs and interviews for selected media, twenty-four hours before his big day. One journalist there was Geoff Green of the *Manchester Evening News*, who had been promised a chat with Jason for all his help with the photographs. The first thing Jason said to Geoff was, "Thanks for what you did for me with the photos, I really appreciate it." Ever since their first meeting they have got on so well and another big plus is that they are both from over the hills in Yorkshire and respect one another!

The day finally arrived, Tuesday 17th October 2000 and I set off early to make final preparations but hit a snag when the road was blocked near Brooklands station due to an accident. Thirty minutes later I was at my desk and my adrenalin was flowing, never mind Robbo's. My mobile went and it was Robbo. I told him about the roadblock and he said, "Swanny, just chill my friend, anyone would think something important was happening."

The press started to arrive from ten o'clock and by quarter

to eleven it was standing room only in the clubhouse.

I waited by the main gate for him and he arrived with his wife Amanda. Deaks took Jason to the front of the room where he sat with Brian Kennedy, Adrian Hadley and Deaks; I found a seat for Amanda at the back. The idea was that Jason likes to keep his family away from the spotlight and nobody could start pestering Amanda or photographing her.

Robbo did well at the conference, answering all the questions thrown at him. Brian talked of his vision for the club as did Deaks and Adrian Hadley, who was Director of Rugby, did a good job answering all the technical questions. The Q & A took over an hour - they normally take ten minutes - then it was one-to-ones and photos, plus television and radio. I got Jason a drink and he whispered, "This is good fun, isn't it?"

"Wait till you go outside, there are a load more journalists waiting who could not get in," I said.

"You're kidding me," he replied.

"I wish I was! Don't forget to give consistent answers. I get all the papers and check them," I said.

Outside, Jason was surrounded by media men wanting a quote and one said, "Where do you live?"

"In a house," was Robbo's reply, again protecting his family.

Next question, "Can we have your mobile phone number in case we need to call you?"

"No, ring Swanny and he will get me to call you back," Robbo said looking at me with a smile.

After the press had left I asked Robbo if he fancied doing Granada Reports live at 6-30pm. "Yeh, why not, let's get them all out of the way today then I can play rugby," he said.

Amanda had gone home because she was attending a

religious gathering at Ribby Hall Caravan Park, north of Preston and Jason was joining her later.

I drove Robbo to Granada, via Burger King and he did his final interview of the day before we headed home.

In the car driving home, Robbo said, "Thanks for today, Swanny, you did a great job, but if everything goes according to plan you could be busier than today for a few years to come."

"Pleasure Robbo, and can I just say that you looked very smart today in your suit and tie."

"Cheers, pal, it's the first time I have worn it since my wedding," he laughed.

I dropped Robbo off at his home in Leyland and he went down the drive, jumped in his car and set off to join Amanda.

Just as I was turning into my drive my mobile rang, "Hey, Swanny, let me know what's in the papers tomorrow, will you?"

Robbo never buys papers, rarely watches television and tells me he only listens to me on the radio!

Robbo's first day training was a real eye opener for him. Remember, he had been playing summer rugby for five seasons and was not used to the wind and rain that winter rugby provided.

He came into my office with Apollo and his new friends Bryan Redpath and Mel Deane asking whether there were any plans to move the game to summer.

Jason's debut was planned for the fifth of November, at home to Coventry in the Tetley's Bitter Cup. Ticket sales were poor and Deaks had an idea to give everyone who came a pint of Tetley's and a pie. The crowd for Jason's debut was under 3,000. A crowd of Wigan fans had made the journey to watch him and told Jason after the game they had come not only to watch him but for the free pies!

"How bad is that Swanny, they even feed the crowd for free and they can only get 3,000, there's a lot to do here!" Jason said.

"I know pal, Steve Hanley is telling me the ground only holds 5,000 and we should be able to fill it," I replied.

Steve has been at the club since the late nineties and always joked about us not filling the ground. When we did and then moved to Edgeley Park, I reminded him of the early days of the Brian Kennedy era.

After the game both Jason and Apollo were invited to the Press Conference and while Robbo was on a high, scoring late in the game, AP was annoyed he had been sinbinned for 'clotheslining' a Coventry player.

"In Rugby League it is termed a slap, I can't believe I got binned for that," AP said.

After the conference Jason started winding up his mate Apollo about the 'tackle' and AP said, "Well, he was asking for it, so I let him sample my forearm."

The following week, Rotherham were the visitors to Heywood Road in the cup and 2,167 turned up to watch. Robbo said, "Swanny the crowds are going down since I signed, soon there will be nobody here and I will have to jump over the fence to get the ball back!"

Brian Kennedy had a vision for the club but he had inherited a squad of players who on the whole were not up to it and paid the price. Nowadays very few remain from the early days.

Carole and I jetted off on a holiday to Mexico's west coast where rugby had never been heard of and there are no papers or British Television to watch. After ten days I was browner than Robbo and as Deaks used to say after a holiday "ten foot high and bullet-proof!"

Jason was hoping to attract some sponsors with his move and they were not forthcoming and one day in December

2000 he said, "Do you know any good agents Swanny? I need some boots."

"Funny you should say that Jase, Laura Bogard who works for Octagon, who look after Zurich's interest in the Premiership asked me to give you this." It was a CD Rom showing Octagon's portfolio.

Robbo took it home and the following day came in and said, "They look okay, can you fix up a meeting for me?" I rang Laura who travelled to Heywood Road with her boss Clifford Bloxham and the deal was done. Over the last five years Octagon and Jason have worked together so well and helped build Jason's profile on the world stage. Jason and I agree that I can look after the Rugby Media but Octagon are the best in their field for player representation.

Early in 2001 St Helens were playing Brisbane Broncos at the Reebok Stadium in Bolton for the World Club Championship Crown. Deaks thought it a good idea for us to go and sorted out some tickets but Robbo didn't fancy driving so I picked him up and along with Carole we drove the short distance to the stadium from Leyland. As we approached it was snowing, raining and blowing a gale. Robbo said, "We will get drenched, where are you parking, Swanny?"

"Leave it to me, I told Super League that I was bringing you and they have allocated me a spot on the official car park," I replied.

"Swanny, if I ever go shopping do you fancy driving me as you never cease to amaze me?" Robbo replied.

Saints won a bruising game and I caught up with Robbo in the lounge on the far side of the ground. As we neared his home, I spotted something lying in the road. I was ready to drive around it but Robbo told me to stop the car.

In the road was a very drunken young man who was out of it. Robbo said, "Give me a lift Swanny," so we picked up the drunk and sat him on a nearby wall.

As we got back in the car Robbo said, "That was me a few years ago and a few people picked me up off the floor I can tell you!" That's the humane side of Robbo who will always help out where he can.

Robbo was soon called up to train with the England team and after Christmas made his debut for England 'A' at Wrexham against Wales. It took twenty-five minutes for him to get a pass and one or two Rugby League journalists were quite sarcastic in their comments of Jason's move to Union.

The following day in the full international at the Millennium Stadium, Dan Luger injured his neck and would be out for several weeks. Robbo rang me on the following Monday and said, "Swanny, guess what, I am on the bench for England against Italy."

His progression and dedication had paid off and Clive Woodward saw the potential in 'Billy Whizz' where others just laughed and said he had "sold his soul to the Union, moved for the money and would regret leaving Rugby League."

As I had done at Wigan, I opened Robbo's mail, and to be honest, some of it was quite sickening to read. Letters from spineless people who never wrote their address or signed the letters, using all sorts of abusive language, probably thinking Robbo would read it. How wrong they were, he never saw any of them. There were some complimentary messages for Jason from people thanking him for his contribution to Rugby League, but sadly they were outweighed by the abuse.

I sat down at home to watch the game against Italy and hoped that Robbo would get a run. Fifty minutes into the game he got his chance when Ben Cohen was replaced by Robbo, wearing number 22. Robbo was soon in the thick of the action but the England players seemed reluctant to pass him the ball. The *Daily Mail* on the Monday following the game had a cartoon with a member of the England backroom team holding up a placard that read "Someone pass the ball to Jason".

The following week Sale Sharks travelled to Northampton and Jason was named at full back for the first time. I believe to this day that full back was where Clive Woodward saw Jason at his best and had had a word with Sale Sharks about it. Sale lost 26-32 but Robbo was outstanding at Full Back, scoring an awesome try.

The following week Jason was back on the bench for England against Scotland in the Calcutta Cup match at Twickenham. England won 43-3 and Robbo was only used for 18 minutes after replacing Mike Catt. In those precious few minutes, he offloaded a great ball to Will Greenwood to send him under the sticks. I spoke to Robbo about his efforts that evening and asked him about the try and what it was like to actually get the ball after his cameo role against Italy. Robbo laughed and said, "I remember offloading and the next thing I remember was lying flat on my back watching a plane come into land and the crowd cheering. Someone copped me with a late shot." Studying the video afterwards, Robbo was taken out by a big Scottish forward about two seconds after he offloaded.

Things were rocking behind the scenes at Heywood Road and while I was out with Jason and Pete Anglesea at a school in Lytham St Annes I received a phone call from Peter Deakin telling me to get Pete and Jason back as soon as possible.

We were all in separate cars, as we had planned to have an early finish and we recreated the 'Wacky Races' going down the three motorways between Lytham and Sale, Jason winning comfortably in his BMW and Pete Anglesea coming second after attempting to drive me off the road. We went into the clubhouse and were told that Adrian Hadley had resigned as Director of Rugby and that Jim Mallinder would be Head Coach with former hooker Steve Diamond returning to the club as his Assistant. 'Mally' had been a great servant to Sale Sharks and his career had ended the previous autumn with a badly broken jaw. Steve Diamond had also been a Sale Sharks stalwart and returned from a spell at Macclesfield. Coach Glen Ross was moved over to player recruitment, as Brian Kennedy was desperate to turn things around after such a promising start to the season had gone badly wrong.

In the final Six Nations game England beat France 48-19, and Robbo again replaced Ben Cohen with 24 minutes of the game remaining. In three matches, Jason had played 72 minutes for England, but the best was yet to come.

A ritual with the England team is that any player who makes his debut has to sing on the team bus. Robbo said, "I sang Saturday Night At The Movies wearing my England blazer, and do you know, Swanny, that's the first time I have had a blazer since I was in the Boys Brigade in Hunslet!"

Sale Sharks' season was moving towards a conclusion with nothing to play for as Rotherham were all ready relegated and Sale Sharks were too far off the pace to challenge for honours.

The newspapers around this time were speculating who would be selected for the British and Irish Lions squad to tour Australia during the summer. One or two journalists were having a punt at the surprise choices and Robbo and I had a laugh as the selection day neared in that the interest in Jason was growing by the day.

Sale Sharks played London Irish at Heywood Road in mid–April under the lights. The lights were originally installed for training in the amateur days of the club and were dim to say the least.

Mid-afternoon I took a call from an Irish gentleman who said that he was a Lions selector and could he have a seat for himself and two colleagues for the game. Cheekily I said, "Who are you looking at tonight?"

"Several players, but one in particular," was the reply. I thought to myself, 'I wonder?' and then as I was busy doing my jobs for the game put it to the back of my mind.

Robbo had the game of his life, cutting the Irish defenders open with his runs from deep and they kept kicking him the ball to bring back!

After the game I caught up with Jason and told him about the guests who had been at the game. He just shrugged his shoulders and said, "Nice thought, Swanny, but I have only played 72 minutes of International Rugby so why would they want me?"

"To sing on the bus!" I replied.

Lions selection is the strangest way of dealing with players I have ever come across. For the 2001 tour they were told by telephone ten minutes before the Press Conference. In 2005 Sir Clive Woodward sent a text to his squad!

The problem on the morning was that Jason was working in his garden on a fence where one of the dogs kept escaping and his mobile phone was in the house.

Peter Jackson rang me and said he was trying to get hold of Jason for a reaction to his selection. I took a deep breath, rang his mobile, no answer: So I rang the house and Amanda answered and I calmly (well as calmly as I could be) asked to speak to Jason.

"Robbo you are on the Lions tour pal, you have done it!" I said

Robbo's reply was, "Great, I will ring you back shortly,"

I came off the phone thinking that I had been more excited than he was!

Ten minutes later my mobile rang. It was Robbo, who was now switched on. "Swanny, that's not bad for a boy from Rugby League, it's incredible news. Do you think I should come down to the ground to talk to the Press?"

I replied, "You set off and I will have them waiting here."

I phoned Simon Wilkinson and Mike Brett who are top photographers, located a Lions top and then rang Geoff Green and the local papers and television and radio stations.

Within an hour we had Robbo being photographed in his Lions top and Heywood Road was bouncing. Sale had two legendary players in Fran Cotton and Steve Smith who had made the Lions but Robbo was the first in the professional era to represent the club.

We had a brew together after the media had gone on their way and Geoff Green stayed behind to chat.

Stuart Barnes, the former Bath and England fly-half and outspoken Sky Sports pundit had said he would eat his hat if Jason went on the Lions Tour. I like Stuart and he plays a good part on Sky Sports' excellent Rugby Union coverage, but he puts his foot in it sometimes and I could not wait to see the weekly magazine show Rugby Club to see what he would say.

I had some good contacts at Sky Sports from my Rugby League days, including Eddie Hemmings, their Rugby League commentator. We hatched a plan to make Stuart Barnes eat his words, but even though Stuart was prepared to hold his hand up and get involved in a televised stunt, the plan did not get off the ground due to resistance from Wigan. I thought it was a PR own goal for Rugby League as the media coverage Jason was attracting could only have boosted Rugby League's profile.

The season ended for Sale Sharks with a dinner at Old Trafford but two weeks later my boss and mate Peter Deakin was taken ill.

Deaks collapsed at an amateur Rugby League game in Oldham and was rushed to hospital. He was released the following day and came into work saying it was gallstones, and that after the Lions trip he would have them removed.

The following day he was taken ill again and had some tests carried out at Warrington Hospital.

I thought there was something strange when he said that he was unable to drive and I became his personal chauffeur, but never asked any questions, as he was his happy smiling self with his usual appetite.

Deaks started to forget things regularly and delegated more than he had ever done in the past (and that was saying something I can tell you).

He would go home from work early and was suffering from headaches most of the day.

We saw less and less of Deaks as the Lions trip neared, and Jim Mallinder and Steve Diamond were trying to sort out their squad for the new season. Fortunately both Brian Kennedy and Ian Blackhurst are not only good businessmen but knowledgeable about Rugby Union and the 2001-2002 squad was starting to be assembled.

As Jason was preparing to leave with the Lions, I was signing for all sorts of parcels for him at work and from well wishers. The main issue was his boots, which were delivered late and I had to take them home for Robbo to pick up. When he called round, he sat in the armchair and up jumped the family pet dog Bazil, a very independent Lhasa Apso. As Robbo went to stroke him Bazil growled at him and showed his full set of teeth. It's the only time I have ever seen Jason frightened in the time I had known him. True to form though, Robbo got up and started darting about side stepping Bazil who thought it was a big game. Since that day though, Jason has never trusted Bazil and to be honest I think Bazil has bitten everyone I know, except Robbo!

The day before Jason left home to join up with the Lions I went to see him, wished him well and he gave me the key to his house saying, "If the alarm goes off Swanny, can you sort it out for me? You have my mobile number and I will give you the hotel numbers for the tour."

"No problem pal, just fetch me a stick of rock and send me a postcard from Oz," I said.

After the team arrived in Australia I got a call from Robbo saying that he had turned his ankle in training and would not feature in the first game of the tour against Western Australia. The Lions won 116-10, scoring eighteen tries! I thought that Robbo's ankle tweak might go against him as the backs had been in great form during the game.

I got a text message the day after which read "Swanny I'm in for the game against Queensland Presidents next Tuesday. Can you video the game for me?"

The game started quietly and I had some office work to do but I had a television in the corner of the office and watched Robbo race in for a five-try debut!

What can you say? I was speechless until my mobile rang and heard Robbo at the other end. "Swanny, I hope you can handle the media calls about today's game, you said we needed to build my Rugby Union profile and the profile of Sale Sharks."

I replied, "You did a good job, a bit like me last night when your alarm went off."

"What happened?"

"We had a thunderstorm and the sound set off your alarm. Can I ask you when was the last time you changed the battery in the alarm system?"

"I haven't," he said.

"No, it was replaced the week before you and Amanda moved in, way back in 1996, it's three years out of date. But don't worry Jason, I was soaking in the bath when the police called." I said.

"What a sight that must have been!" he laughed, "anyway, Swanny, I have to go now, can you let me know what the press have to say about today's game?" he finished.

I was lucky my mobile phone was fully charged as I took so many calls from rugby writers worldwide asking a variety of questions on Robbo. Jason always joked that if there was ever a quiz about his rugby career, I should enter it, as I'd easily win!

The following day it was wall-to-wall Robbo with every paper carrying his picture and kind words. Even some of the non-Jason believers, were beginning to warm to him and one even backtracked so far as to say Jason should be considered for the Test Team!

Robbo was rested for the next game, but was not happy with the intensity of the training, saying it was a 'killer'.

You can always tell when Robbo isn't playing, as he gets up to mischief. One morning about eight o'clock the phone rang in my office and a voice asked for me personally. The voice went on to ask whether the caravan Carole and I had was for rent as he wanted to book it for six of his family and four cats! I was just about to lose it and tell the caller to go forth and multiply when the voice at the other end cracked and said, "Swanny, it's me, Robbo, I got you that time pal, even my room-mate thought it was funny."

Good job it was Robbo, I felt like one of those people caught out by Jeremy Beadle. It was also a good job I saw the funny side as Robbo is not a fan of swearing!

The following week Australia A beat the Lions and some of the media were having a real go at the Lions. The next game, which was Robbo's second in four days, the Lions regrouped and beat the Waratahs 41-24. Playing for the Warathas was Stuart Pinkerton who was joining Sale Sharks a month later, so as well as watching Robbo score his eighth try in three

FIRST TASTE OF CAPTAINCY Hunslet Boys Club

AN EARLY SWANNY STUNT
Jason and Aussie Willie Peters posing in kilts before Wigan play Gateshead Thunder at Tynecastle, home of Hearts FC, August 1999

THE MASTER
Wigan coach John Monie

CHANGING CODES
Jason, Simon Haughton and Andy Farrell, Wigan greats who all tried Rugby Union

FLOORING THEM
Jason powers through for Wigan, leaving two defenders sprawling

SHEDDING BLOOD
Jason with a bloody nose for troubles

JJB COVER STAR
Jason on the front cover of the JJB Stadium debut programme 1999.

SWOTTING UP
Jason takes a crash
course in Rugby Union
Laws with the help
of namesake Derek
Robinson's book

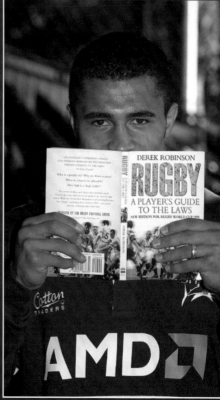

A WARRIOR BECOMES A SHARK
Jason at Sale Sharks' Heywood Road after switching from League to Union, November 2000

DEBUT FIREWORKS
Jason and Apollo Perelini make their debuts for Sale v Coventry, Tetley's Bitter Cup, November 5th 2000

SALE SHARKS

AMD Duron

PROUD MAIN CLUB SPONSOR

Sale Sharks v Coventry
Sunday 5th November 2000 Kick-off 3pm
Tetley's Bitter Cup Round Four

Match Sponsor: Mike India 5

£2

DEBUT POSTER
Jason and Apollo Perelini advertise Sale v Coventry, Tetley's Bitter Cup, November 5th 2000

EAT MY HAT
Former England fly-half, now Sky Sports pundit Stuart Barnes promises to eat his hat if Jason is a success in Rugby Union

HEY STUMPY
Is Bryan Redpath really shorter than Jason?

CROSS CODE CHALLENGE
Apollo Perelini and Jason, opponents in the 2000 Super League Grand Final, team up as Sale Sharks beat St Helens 41-39 in a unique half Union, half League match on January 27th 2003

REUNITED
Jason embraces Inga Tuigamala following Sale's cup defeat at Newcastle Falcons, January 2001

ENGLAND DEBUT
The Daily Mail's view of Jason's England debut v Italy, February 17th 2001

REPLACEMENT
Jason came on for Ben Cohen to make his England debut v Italy, February 17th 2001

JASON & JONNY
Robinson and Wilkinson,
England's two best-
known stars

CAPTAIN OF ENGLAND
Jason urges on his England team-mates

ACTION MAN
France, February 2005

A WORLD CUP HERO RETURNS
Jason runs out at Edgeley Park for the first match after the World Cup triumph to face Cardiff Blues in the Heineken Cup, December 2003

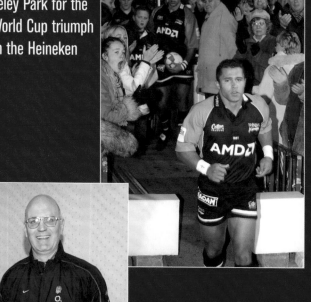

WEBB ELLIS TROPHY
Jason keeps both hands firmly on the World Cup as Swanny looks on at Edgeley Park, December 2003

WORLD CUP WOODWARD
Sir Clive shows off the Webb Ellis Trophy at Edgeley Park, December 2003

DIRTY BOKS: A nasty bruising encounter with South Africa saw England win 53-3, November 2002

SAFE: Jason catches a high ball against South Africa

GRAND SLAM: Jason swaps shirts after clinching the Six Nations and Grand Slam against Ireland at Lansdowne Road, March 2003

JASON THE LION
Jason rounds future Sale team-mate Stu Pinkerton to score for the Lions v NSW Waratahs, June 2001

TRIES FOR FUN
Jason scored ten tries on his first Lions tour, including two in the Tests

ANOTHER TRY
Jason beats George Gregan to the line in the third Test v Australia, July 2001

EUROPEAN SEMI
Jason hands off Terry Fanolua as Sale Sharks beat Gloucester 28-27 at Northampton to reach the Parker Pen European Shield final, April 2002

TACKLED
Jason gets stuck in to Gloucester

OXFORD FINAL

Jason in action as Sale Sharks beat Pontypridd 25-22 to win the Parker Pen
European Shield final at Oxford's Kassam Stadium, May 2002

EUROPEAN SHIELD
Jason holds the Parker Pen European Shield aloft watched by Club Doctor Dave Jones, April 2002

FORTY WINKS
Jason gets his head down during a photo shoot

CHAMPAGNE CHARLIE
Jason celebrates with fellow England
international Charlie Hodgson

TOP TEAM
Sale Sharks celebrates the win
at Oxford, May 2002

games I was interested in our new signing. Unfortunately the game exploded with Duncan McRae being sent off for a vicious assault on Ronan O'Gara.

Robbo told me in confidence that he had been selected for the First Test but it was not common knowledge so I sat on it until the team was announced and the media went into overdrive.

Jason being away with the Lions threw up a great opportunity for Carole and I in the form of a trip to Wimbledon for the tennis. Octagon, Jason's representation, handle several tennis players and had some tickets spare for one day's play. We parked the car at Stanmore and had just boarded the underground train when my mobile phone rang. It was Jason, on the eve of his Lions Test debut, ringing to check everything was okay and that we were on the way to Wimbledon. That's the sort of bloke he is though, and as he said in his autobiography, "We are good for one another."

His Lions debut was incredible – after only two minutes the ball was passed to Jason who beat Chris Latham to score in the corner. He had so little space to work in that I have viewed the try over and over wondering how he managed to stay in the field of play.

The Lions won the game 29-13 and for the second time in three weeks the newspapers and media were full of pictures of the 'Rugby League Convert' playing a starring role for the Lions. I still maintain to this day that Robbo should have scored another try had one of his glory-merchant teammates passed to him near the line instead of taking the the wrong option.

There is nothing worse than a wounded Aussie and in Melbourne a week after the First Test the Lions were beaten 35-14 with Jonny Wilkinson leaving the pitch on a stretcher.

Sale Sharks owner Brian Kennedy flew out for the final

game and Deaks rang me from Australia asking me to see if I could get BK some tickets. I contacted Jason, Octagon and the RFU and it was Jason who saved the day wheeling and dealing with his team-mates so Brian Kennedy and Ian Blackhurst could see the game.

The Lions were patched up for the series decider, the Third Test and lost 29-23, with Robbo touching down for the tenth time on the tour and finishing as the leading try scorer.

I waited for the phone to ring and a couple of hours later Robbo told me he was shattered and that both his Achilles were giving him a lot of pain. He told me he was travelling up to Cairns on the North East Coast with Amanda and Cameron for a break before coming home.

"Keep in touch Robbo, you ring me if you need anything but just go and chill out."

"Chill Out? You're joking Swanny it's one of the hottest places in the world and even I will need some serious sun block!"

Peter Deakin returned home and rang me to ask me to call round to his home with his mail and any paperwork that needed his attention. He sounded very distant but I thought it was the jet lag.

When I called at his home he answered the door and invited me in. "Swanny, you know that scan I had at Warrington? It has highlighted two patches and the specialist thinks they may be tumours. I am going into hospital on Thursday for tests, so can you let everyone know at work?"

I felt numb; here was the guy who took me to Warrington and then Sale who was clearly not well.

On the way home I rang Apollo and broke radio silence with Robbo in Cairns. Robbo was upset when I told him and said he would say a prayer for Deaks, whom he thought a lot of. Deaks had been a big player in getting Jason to sign for the Sharks.

I visited Deaks in hospital with Apollo and Adam Jude and he was upbeat. While I was there he signed a letter of appointment for my young son Dan who had just left school and was joining the club to work on the administrative side of the business. Peter had promised Dan a job after he had done some work experience with the club and had been impressed with his work ethic. "Swanny, you should be proud of him, he is a real grafter and will be a big asset." Dan had not done too well with his school exams but fitted in perfectly when he joined the club and was respected by everyone.

Robbo rang every day for an update on Peter's health and we were all surprised that Deaks returned to work in between his chemotherapy treatment sessions.

SILVERWARE FOR SHARKS

We had the pre-season Press day at Heywood Road but we didn't have a good turn out from the media because Leicester Tigers had decided to have their event on the same day. I was not happy with this but Robbo sat me down after the event and said, "Swanny, keep doing what you do well and the media will see it the Sale Shark's way eventually." Here was Jason Robinson giving me media advice!

Jim Mallinder and Steve Diamond had worked the marketplace with signings including Kevin Yates, Stuart Turner, Iain Fullarton and Stuart Pinkerton. James Wade had worked wonders with the Jets (Shark's second team) with players like Mark Cueto, Chris Jones and Anthony Elliott making the grade alongside Charlie Hodgson and Andy Titterrell who had been given their debut the previous season.

My son Dan coming to join us on the staff posed a small problem, in that everyone at the club had a nickname. Jason was Robbo or Billy Whizz, Apollo was AP, Mark Cueto was Frank and so on, but had Dan been called 'Swanny' you would have got two for the price of one. In Dan's first week the players were eating in the clubhouse and I joined Jason and Apollo. Suddenly Apollo said, "That's it! Dan can be called Cygnet as he is the small Swan!" Robbo thought it was a great idea and the nickname was adopted by Dan, who was pleased to be "one of the lads."

The season started with a friendly against Worcester, which was staged as stalwart Dave Baldwin's benefit game. Robbo had only been back a week from Australia but insisted on turning out for Dave. Less than 1,000 people turned up and Robbo turned on the style with a quality performance from full back but a young man called Mark Cueto stole the show with a fantastic hat-trick, and since that day Mark has been the Sharks' right wing. It was interesting on the day, as Mark ran Worcester ragged with a hat-trick, that Jason was spending time during the game to coach and encourage Mark, who is the first to say that Jason has been a big influence on him. Playing for Worcester on that hot August day was Kingsley Jones, who Philippe Saint Andre brought to Sale Sharks three years later as Head Coach.

The first game of the Zurich Premiership season was away to Bristol and Sale Sharks won 35-25. On the same weekend Newcastle opened their account with a good win over Leicester Tigers at Kingston Park. However, instead of celebrating with his team, Falcons boss Rob Andrew told the press that while he was happy with the win their next game was at Heywood Road against Sale, and if they lost that game it would be like the England football team losing to Albania! What could we say at Sale Sharks? Brian Kennedy thought it was excellent motivation for the Sharks and Rob Andrew's remarks were photocopied and blu-tacked to the dressing room walls. The players were hyper all week and couldn't wait to get on the field. The only person not taking a blind bit of notice of all the hype was Jason, who had seen it all before and preferred his rugby to do the talking. A crowd just short of 5,000 jammed into Heywood Road and we were delighted that England Head Coach Clive Woodward made the trip to watch the game.

The Sharks won 37-11, Jonny Wilkinson left the action in the first half after a thundering tackle by Apollo Perelini and Robbo scored a trademark try. After the game the media quizzed Rob Andrew about his remarks about Albania, but he took it all in his stride. Robbo caught up with his big friend Inga Tuigamala, now playing for Newcastle, who had rescued him from the scrap heap at Wigan when Robbo's life was spiralling out of control. He introduced me to Inga, who really is a larger than life character.

The following Tuesday, the World witnessed the terrifying events in New York on television and Robbo was in my office at the time. We were all shocked by the events as they unfolded on the screen but Jason kept his own counsel, obviously shocked but bottling it all up inside. In crisis situations like this, Jason becomes very private and I am sure he speaks to the great man in the sky for guidance. The one thing that has always struck me about Jason's religious beliefs is that he is not a 'Bible basher' and does not go round trying to convert everyone he sees. The perception in his media interviews for years is that he is a man who reads nothing but the Bible and spends all his off-field time praying which is wrong and one of the main reasons I am attempting to show the 'Real Jason Robinson' in this book.

The Friday after the Newcastle victory I was standing at the fax machine when a report came through. Newcastle had cited Pete Anglesea for an incident in which Jon Dunbar of Newcastle had received an eye injury.

The following game was away to Wasps at Loftus Road, which Sale Sharks won 40-21 with Jason scoring another top-drawer try, but the Sharks crashed back to earth the following week when Philippe Saint Andre's Gloucester battered the Sharks 44-21 at Heywood Road.

Pete Anglesea was due at the disciplinary committee meeting the following week and we were all in shock when he received a twelve-month ban. The club got behind Peter 100%, with his team-mates and officials attempting to keep his spirits up. Jason had a quiet chat with Big Red (Pete's nickname) and even though Pete is one opponent you would hate to meet on a pitch, he was clearly shaken.

The first game of Pete Anglesea's ban was the 93-0 win over Roma where both he and Jason Robinson acted as bottle carriers. Apollo scored a hat-trick of tries and Richard Wilks bagged a couple as well, filling in for Pete at flanker. I chatted with Jason and Pete on the sidelines and as Pete was quietly watching the game I said, "Blimey, Pete, even you would have scored this afternoon." Robbo was bent double laughing and thankfully Pete saw the funny side. I won't print what he said, but it wasn't the sort of language you would use at a Parish Garden Party.

Brian Kennedy stepped in and was instrumental in organising Pete's defence. Club Chairman Quentin Smith organised the legal team and off they went to Twickenham to appeal against the ban. Peter won his appeal and things returned to normal as his team-mates dropped the sympathy and re-introduced the great team spirit that was a major plus with the squad. Kevin Yates appeared at training wearing goggles, but Pete, being a quick-witted 'Wiganer', responded by wearing industrial earmuffs, a reminder of Kevin's ban when he was at Bath. Despite the fact that the incident at Bath cost Kevin international honours, Yatesy laughed it off.

My son Dan was sharing my office and as I had to buy all the papers every day, Dan used to have a look though them after I had cut the Sale Sharks mentions out. Within weeks of moving in with me, Dan had the office wall-to-wall Kylie Minogue, that was until Jason came in to sign some autograph cards and looked around. He disappeared with Dan for about ten minutes and when Dan returned he stood on the furniture with a staple remover taking down his Kylie collection. I don't know what Robbo said to Dan but from that day on he started to read papers from back to front rather than diving for page three every morning!

Dan had suffered because of my divorce in 1994 and I was pleased that I was able to spend some quality time with him.

Divorces are rarely amicable and I missed spending time with Dan during his formative years. I think Jason saw a lot of his younger self in Dan and took him under his wing and I must say that Dan has matured so much thanks to his time at Sale Sharks. Robbo is *the man* when it comes to stash (rugby collectibles) and he kitted Dan out with some British Lions training gear and a Lions jersey.

Jason's personal Lions success brought its spin-offs, one of which was a limited edition print run of photos taken by David Rogers. The picture was of Robbo scoring his first test try for the Lions. I organised one of the suites at Heywood Road with Tracy Grady, the Conference and Banqueting Manager, for Robbo to sit down and sign a thousand pictures. David Rogers is one of the best photographers around and he and Jason chatted for a couple of hours as the photos were signed. Jason never rushes his signature, not even after a game when he is surrounded by hundreds of rugby supporters. It's a work of art but he has perfected it over the years and it is nearly impossible to copy.

In October Sale Sharks lost 17-20 away to Bath or should I say Sale Sharks lost to Matt Perry? The day did not go well as Kevin Yates was sinbinned for a high tackle on his old team-mate Mike Catt and even though Sale Sharks kept a win in their sights they could not edge ahead. I had gone to the Super League Grand Final with Carole and during the first half Bradford Bulls were demolishing Wigan, scoring almost a point a minute. Robbo wanted updating by text message as his Rugby League heart would always be with Wigan. At one stage he replied to one of my texts by texting me with the words "I should be passing Old Trafford at half time, do you think I would get a game off the bench?" I texted back, "Go home Robbo, there's nothing even you can do here."

The following week Jason was with England in Dublin to complete the previous season's Six Nations, which was curtailed due to the foot and mouth outbreak. This game was Jason's first start for England having played 72 minutes in three games before the Lions tour. Not a game to remember though, as a Keith Wood try saw off the England challenge.

Next up were the Autumn Internationals where Robbo was commuting to and from Pennyhill Park, Bagshot, which is the England training base. Robbo had an arrangement with Clive Woodward that he was able to take Amanda, his son Cameron and daughter Jemima with him, as he hates being away from home. I am not surprised, with the amount of time the team spend at Bagshot. I could never understand why the team never had a Midlands based training base. The journey was 250 miles from Jason's home and goodness knows what Jonny Wilkinson felt like commuting from the North East. The trip usually started on a Sunday evening, a good night's sleep and then training Monday and Tuesday before driving back North for training on Wednesday.

After his personal Lions success, Jason received invitations from all over the country to attend religious events, prize-giving ceremonies and dinners, most of which he turned down due to lack of time. We got to a stage where we had a standard letter saved in Microsoft Word and while Jason would have liked to have attended more, giving boy scouts their certificates in Bournemouth on a Thursday night was not really practical. Most people accepted the letter apologising but some took offence and would ring me up and give me abuse down the phone. In the early days I used to relay people's comments to Jason but eventually I asked him if he had any time spare and worked in personal appearances where I was able to. To the abusive callers I designed a system to deal with them which I will patent one day!

Requests for Charity Donations went into overdrive too, with over fifty letters a week arriving from all over the country. Each letter received was read by me and I shortlisted a few letters to discuss with Robbo. We sent out shirts, shorts, socks and boots as well as posters and programmes, but sadly some of the items sent by Jason in good faith finished up on Internet auction sites. I would not say Jason became angry with this, more disillusioned. In later years I found out that Jonny Wilkinson's father logs everything that Jonny signs and can track items back to the source. The action we took was that Jason would only sign items sent in if they were personalised to an individual. Even then people tried to get around this by stating it was being auctioned for some life-threatening Charity, but after a meeting of minds Jason and I decided to send letters of intent that the items would be personalised *after* the event.

Life had changed so much since the days in Hilton Street, Wigan, but I always kept on top of Robbo's mailbag, even though some signing sessions took two or more hours, but then again Robbo always bought lunch!

The Autumn Internationals opened with England playing Romania, which was one of the biggest mismatches of all time. England won 134-0 and Robbo bagged four tries. Young Charlie Hodgson made his England debut and scored an incredible 43 points. Back at Heywood Road, Leicester Tigers were mauling Sale Sharks 37-3. I drove home after the Sharks defeat and watched Robbo warm the Twickenham crowd with his incredible side steps and dummies. Until this game Jason was just an England player but I think this was the game where he won over the crowd, in that every time he touched the ball thereafter, there was a gasp of expectation.

The Autumn Internationals and travelling were making Robbo weary and to compound problems, his first game back with the Sharks was in London, away to Harlequins. Sharks won this game but Harlequins gained revenge by beating the Sharks in the Powergen Cup in December, in extra time. There was a blessing in disguise in that part of the Heywood Road ground was frozen solid, causing the postponement of the game against Leeds Tykes which gave Robbo a few days off.

Training resumed on Boxing Day for the big game against runaway leaders Leicester Tigers the next day. While enjoying a Christmas get-together at home, the phone rang and it was Robbo asking me to take his new sponsored car down to Leicester to enable him to get away early and spend some time with his family.

"You know, Swanny, I am thinking of buying a big picture of me to put over the fireplace so the kids know who their dad is!" he said.

Robbo asked me to pick him up at seven the following morning so en route I picked up Dan who fancied a ride in a 'top of the range' car.

When I arrived at Robbo's house on the outskirts of Leyland he had overslept and came to the door in a tee shirt and boxers! I only wish I had taken a camera with me to share the frightening sight that greeted me!

Twenty minutes later we were on the way to Heywood Road to get Robbo on the team coach. He gave me a crash course in driving the car and advised me it performed better in top gear. When we arrived at the ground Robbo demolished a full English breakfast before setting up the on-board navigator with the Leicester Tigers postcode.

"Remember Swanny, don't answer it back and follow the instructions the nice lady gives you," he said.

We had a trial run and I shouted, "Robbo, how do you turn that lady's voice off, she sounds like my ex-wife!"

"You can't and by the way the boot is full of Cadbury's chocolate from my sponsors, so eat what you want," he laughed.

Dan leapt over the seat and was amazed that there was a full

Cadbury range and started demolishing Flakes and Whole Nut bars.

Lisa Robinson, who runs the club shop, came with us as she had never visited Welford Road. Lisa was the only one who had been with the club longer than me and is a good friend. She also has a great working relationship with Robbo and is about the only person I know who can get Robbo to model merchandise.

We followed the coach towards the M56 but I knew a quicker way to the M6, unbeknown to the onboard navigator. My phone soon rang and it was Robbo telling me to do as the lady told me otherwise I would get lost!

Leicester Tigers at Welford Road is a daunting task. The partisan crowd are incredible but they recognise good play by opponents and applaud it. Robbo scored an incredible try that left Geordan Murphy clutching at thin air. That, however, was as good as it got and the Tigers won 33-10. The Sharks were second in the table at the time but had to bow to the superior Tigers side.

After the game Robbo signed autographs for everyone in the queue before we set off home. He decided the M1 was the fastest way home, cutting across to Stoke on the A500. I thought this was very impressive thinking by him until we came to a roundabout and Robbo was rubbing his chin.

"People, on my right is McDonald's and on my left is Burger King, what's it going to be?" he asked.

Dan chirped up, "Let's do both, Jason, you can do it!"

Robbo just laughed and the vote said Burger King.

In we walked and the guy behind the counter was shocked to see the current England full back walking in with three friends and ordering huge meals.

Robbo said, "This is the staff party, people, so put on your party hats!"

We sat there demolishing the meals and Robbo then said,

"Swanny, I am doing okay with sponsors but I could really do with a KFC Gold Card where I can have as many portions of chicken and chips as I want!"

He was serious too; in fact, there are five words you will never hear him say and they are, "I can't eat any more."

Robbo was winding Dan up saying, "Food like this is fuel for my body and I can do eighty minutes to a meal from here."

Jason was in such a great mood and told me that Jim Mallinder had given him some games off to rest while he did his commuting to Bagshot in readiness for the Six Nations.

Sale Sharks made it six out of six in their Parker Pen Shield Group and Robbo's next game was against Bristol at Heywood Road in the Shield quarter-final. Jim Mallinder named Robbo at centre and he had a great game on a bitterly cold night.

After the game I bade Jason goodbye as I was going to Barbados for a week to get some sun on my back. His face was a picture. "You're having a laugh, you've only just been on holiday. I am going to have to start going on the sunbed to keep up with you, Swanny."

Robbo started the Six Nations with two tries in the Calcutta Cup game in Edinburgh. A win against Ireland followed before the England wheels fell off with defeat in Paris against the French, although Robbo scored a trademark try from an impossible situation.

Back to Sale and things were going well with wins at home to Bath and Wasps but in the win over Wasps, Robbo injured his groin causing him to miss the England game against Wales. He had intensive physio, he hated missing games but had to concede defeat after a fitness test in which he almost broke my fingers and shattered Dan's watch. He needed some kicking practice and asked Dan and me to field balls he booted down the Heywood Road pitch. I caught his first kick then it was Dan's turn. He did well and caught the ball but broke his watch in the process. "Don't worry, Dan, I'll get you another from the 'Looky Looky' man on my holidays!"

I laughed and then Robbo launched a huge kick and I got in position to catch it but the wind blew the ball off course and it bent back my fingers.

"What was that?" Robbo asked. "I can kick them a lot higher than that, anyway, let's have some lunch."

His groin was giving him pain but he went to his car and produced a sponsor's watch for Dan who was still trying to put his own watch back together.

"How's your fingers, Swanny?" he asked.

"Sore," I replied.

"Well at least it's your left hand and you write with your right hand," he laughed.

Rugby players, I have learned, have no sympathy when you hurt yourself but at least Robbo said it with a smile.

His groin healed and he made his England comeback in Rome as England cruised past Italy, scoring his fourth try of the series. Sale Sharks beat Bristol the following week 53-47 to which Robbo joked, "I think we need to work on defence next week."

By this time Peter Deakin had returned to work on a part-time basis but he was keen to get back into a Chief Executive role and his good friend Nigel Wray of Saracens offered him his old job back at Vicarage Road. Deaks decided to go and the lads all thanked him for his efforts. Before he left the ground, Deaks thanked me for everything and ruffled Dan's hair, telling him to keep up the good work.

At the end of April it was the Parker Pen Shield semi-final against Gloucester at Northampton, and if some of the papers were to be believed, Sale Sharks were just there to make up the numbers. I drove Jason's car to the game with Dan, together with injured players Andy Titterrell, Scott Lines and Vaughan Going. It was a dream to drive the 'week-old car' and I tested it out down the M6 and M1. Robbo had kindly filled it with fuel and I thought the least I could do was test drive it for him!

The game started and Gloucester set off like a house on fire and I thought that this might be as far as we were going in the Parker Pen Shield. Matters got worse when Robbo was taken out collecting a high kick and he spent several minutes flat out on the turf while club doctor David Jones and physiotherapist Michelle Sinclair brought him back into the land of the living.

Sharks won the game courtesy of an incredible penalty miss by Ludovic Mercier in injury time. On the whistle we all ran onto the field to congratulate the players but Robbo looked decidedly worse for wear and coughed up some blood.

I asked him if he was okay and he replied, "Swanny I have felt better but there was no way I was coming off the field."

Robbo took his time getting changed and I found an escape route to the lounge where the players were eating to avoid him having to sign autographs. The job of planning escape routes had become my job more and more as the season wore on as Robbo was running on fumes most of the time.

Jason asked Jim Mallinder for permission to leave the celebrations, as he wanted to get home. Apollo Perelini joined Dan and myself and we hit the road. I offered to drive but Robbo said he wanted to take his mind off his big hit and drive. Once clear of the M1 Robbo was hungry so we pulled into Hilton Park services. I thought we would be having a sandwich but no, our pocket dynamo Billy Whizz headed straight for Burger King. I asked if he should be eating fast food but Robbo replied, "Swanny, Burger King, McDonalds and KFC are rocket fuel for my system and I am running on low so what are we having?"

We all got a tray full of food and sat down in a corner out of sight, or so we thought! In walked Sale Sharks owners Brian Kennedy and Ian Blackhurst.

Brian said, "Does Marty Hulme [Sharks Conditioner] know you eat burgers?"

Robbo replied, "Oh yes, there is no problem." I looked at Jason and smiled and was astonished to see the box of fries had disappeared from view!"

When Brian had gone I said, "You call me Pinocchio for telling lies - often on your behalf - and here you are hiding your chips from Brian Kennedy!"

Apollo chirped in, "Swanny, Brian is a very successful businessman and we are putting some money back into his business."

"How do you work that out?" I asked.

"Burger King, BK... Brian Kennedy, he owns the place," Apollo replied.

I thought to myself that maybe this was not the first time AP and Robbo had been caught out.

After demolishing everything on the tray, Robbo decided he wanted some sweets for the remainder of the journey and headed to the 'Pick'n'Mix' stand in the gift shop.

While queuing to pay, a Sharks fan approached Jason for an autograph for her son who was standing next to her. She pulled a magazine from the rack for Jason to rest on and Robbo said, "I am not resting on that!"

It was a 'top-shelf' men's magazine and the lady had to be content with an autograph on a piece of till roll provided by the cashier.

Robbo never preaches but he has some very high principles and will not budge for anyone.

Walking back to the car, AP and I tried to make light of it but Robbo was shaking his head. "How bad was that? What sort of example does that set to that youngster?"

I saw his point but explained that seeing a British Lion in a motorway service station probably made that lady's day. To this day Robbo has no real idea how big a profile he has.

Sale Sharks' win at Franklins Gardens in the semi-final gave the whole club a massive boost and the last three League games against London Irish, Leeds Tykes and Harlequins were won easily to give the Sharks runners-up spot in the Zurich Premiership.

The following Sunday, Wasps were beaten in the play-offs at Heywood Road but the gate was only 3,283, a week before the Parker Pen Shield final. The Sale Sharks success story was still in its infancy and there was much to do. Robbo used to remark that if he walked down the street in London he would get mobbed for autographs but he could walk freely around Sale and nobody knew him! He used to joke, "Swanny, you are failing here and you need to work on my profile more!"

I just laughed and said that the people down South were easily pleased and Northerners took their time.

Young Rob McEvoy was working single-handed in the ticket office selling final tickets and my son Dan gave Rob a lift selling coach places for the journey to the Kassam Stadium, Oxford United's new ground. It was an explosive combination but both did a great job in selling 4,000 tickets and filling almost 50 coaches.

Jason received some startling news in the days running up to the final - startling was his word, not mine - he had been named Premiership player of the year. Jason was obviously delighted and said that he had not done badly for a lad who had just moved over to Union from Rugby League. While Robbo was chuffed, he was equally delighted for Charlie Hodgson who was named as the Premiership's young player of the year. Charlie had had a great season and the game had rewarded him for his efforts.

The day before the final Dan got his comeuppance from three of the players. I had told him he should be careful about winding up rugby players and as Jason and I were going through some mail, Kevin Yates, Stuart Turner and Pete Anglesea came into my office smiling. They pinned Dan down on the floor, smothered him in hair gel and aftershave. Robbo said as Dan got off the floor, "Told you not to be cheeky to the forwards."

Dan exploded and squared up to Kevin Yates. Not a good idea that, so I put my arm around Dan's shoulders and calmed him down.

On the day of the final Dan and I drove down in pouring rain, thinking, "this might not be the Sharks day – they're great on a flat pitch but the wet may suit Pontypridd better." The rain was so bad on the motorway that I missed the turn-off and had to drive across country from Northampton to Oxford. Nice run, you might say, but not past Silverstone on the weekend of the Superbikes!

We arrived at the Kassam Stadium and picked up our accreditation from the office. We mixed with the press, which is always a good idea before a game as you can sometimes give them a lead to develop. I have always prided myself in getting the media onside and owe this to John Monie and his days at Wigan.

Pontypridd were up for the game and were 15-0 ahead in the first half before Sharks woke up. Steve Hanley received a bad cut to his mouth and I had to stand guard on the dressing room door while the doctor stitched him up.

While standing guard my mobile rang; it was Carole who had gone to St Annes-on-Sea, flat hunting. She had found a great place and wanted to bounce the idea off me. Steve Hanley and I still laugh about it today - there he was being stitched and Swanny was on the door buying a flat!

Sale Sharks received the rounds of the kitchen sink at half

time from coaches Jim Mallinder and Steve Diamond and the second half saw a different Sale Sharks on the pitch.

Martin Shaw, Steve Hanley and Dan Harris scored the tries and the Sharks landed their first major trophy in their 141-year history.

After the game, Robbo requested that he be excused from the pub-crawl the players had planned and we drove back up the motorway with the trophy in the boot of the car.

"Tell you one thing Swanny, you could serve a lot of sandwiches on that Shield. Is it silver?" Robbo asked.

"Solid silver and worth about £12,000 so don't get any ideas, pal," I replied.

Dan and Robbo went into jovial conversation about melting it down and I just concentrated on driving.

We stopped off at Hilton Park for Burger King, what else, and arrived back at Heywood Road where the celebrations had started. We went into the clubhouse and let the fans have a look at the trophy before setting off home.

The following evening the Gala Dinner was held in a marquee on the pitch at Heywood Road and I was delighted to receive an award from Brian Kennedy for my efforts in building the Sharks profile. When the award was being made the whistling started, led by Robbo, who was the first to come over and shake my hand. Club Sponsors AMD gave me a new laptop computer for all the work I had done in getting their brand name across. I felt so proud as this was the first time in any sport my efforts had been rewarded.

Unbelievably the day after I received a call from Wigan Rugby League Club asking me to come down to see Maurice Lindsay for a chat about returning to the club. I declined, but thanked them for thinking about me.

I told Robbo about the call and he just smiled and said, "You should have told them to ring me as your agent and I would have scared them off with the asking price for your services."

I told Jason that I had sweated blood at Wigan but not half as much as I had done for Brian Kennedy and that BK respected the effort people put in and I knew that the Sharks were going places and wanted to be part of it.

With crowds ever on the increase Brian Kennedy was looking at alternative venues as Heywood Road could only ever hold 6,000 at best. He was investing heavily and always planned for the club to be a 'stand alone', rather than relying on him funding it.

Bury Football Club's Gigg Lane ground entered the equation and BK asked several of us to go to there as a working party to have a look at what the ground offered. I must say I was impressed but when we reported back, the fans had got wind of a potential move and had made their thoughts known. Brian invited some fans to come to his offices in Wilmslow, along with members of Trafford Council and told everyone straight that although the club were Zurich Premiership runners-up, Parker Pen Shield Winners and had qualified for the prestigious Heineken Cup, he was losing over a million pounds a season and this could not go on indefinitely.

At one of the meetings I was introduced to Niels de Vos, who was the brains behind the Marketing at the Commonwealth Games in Manchester. Brian told everyone at the meeting that Niels was coming on board as Chief Executive to move the club forward to the next platform.

After the meeting finished Niels asked me about the possibility of me speaking to Jason about him playing in the rugby sevens at the tournament.

I told Niels that Joe Lydon [England Sevens Coach] had spoken to Jason and that he had dug his heels in and said there was no way he was playing.

Niels got more and more involved in the business and his

input and leadership helped us prepare for the 2002-2003 season which was to be our last at Heywood Road.

During the summer break Robbo decided to buy a caravan, but not until he had us all falling about laughing.

Apollo Perelini told me that Robbo had hired a camper van and had driven it home, only to find it untidy on the interior and in need of a wash on the outside. While cleaning the inside, the outside was being jet washed and AP told me there was a noise inside and Robbo had got soaked… the camper van had sprung a leak. Not happy, Robbo took it back and got a refund. Unperturbed, he went out and bought a five-berth caravan and took the family down to Devon and Cornwall for a break. Robbo called me to tell me he was thoroughly enjoying it as he had only been recognised once and was moving freely from site to site.

When he returned home, he became a fully paid-up member of the Caravan Club of Great Britain, which gave us enough 'wind-up' material to last us ages. Robbo was proud of his new purchase though and explained that it was a nice change from visiting hotels and talking rugby with people. I suggested he travel to Jamaica where he would blend in and no one would recognise him. He replied, "The only problem is that if I did, it will be the rainy season so I will have to go when I retire." Robbo likes a drop of sun and I always wind him up well in advance when I go for my annual Caribbean fix!

The news soon escaped that he was a 50 mph caravan driver and he was invited to open the Caravan Show at the G-Mex in Manchester. He wouldn't tell anyone when he was going as he thought we would pay him a visit at the opening ceremony. He was right too, as club jokers Pete Anglesea, Mark Cueto and Steve Hanley did everything to find out the time of his ribbon-cutting appearance!

Sian Masterton, who works for Octagon and looks after

Jason's business interests, rang me before the new season started and told me that Jason was going to write an auto-biography with the view to launching it prior to the 2003 World Cup. Sian told me that *Mail on Sunday* journalist Malcolm Folley had been asked to write the book with Jason. I received a phone call from Malcolm shortly afterwards whereby I set about making a list of people he could speak to. I spoke to Robbo and asked who he wanted Malcolm to speak to as I thought this was the correct thing to do.

Jason's previous life has been well documented in his auto-biography *Finding My Feet* and when I sat down to write this book I did not see the need to visit the time before I knew Robbo personally. Half the stories that circulated then, and still do, to some extent beggar belief anyway.

I was asked to source some photographs for the book and did this for Jason and Sian. To this day the publishers have never said thank you for the effort I put in on their behalf, sourcing photos and telephone numbers for people to interview. I also set up two signing sessions for the book on the launch day and it was just taken for granted by them. Malcolm Folley is a well-respected writer and I was amazed that, having helped Jason write his book, he should write an exclusive about Jason in his paper at the end of the 2003-2004 season, but more of that later.

HEYWOOD ROAD TO EDGELEY PARK

The 2002-2003 season began with a Press Conference and I was delighted that all newspapers were represented, unlike the previous season. Heywood Road was a media circus with the press wanting to talk to coaches Jim Mallinder and Steve Diamond as well as the players. The media operation at Sale Sharks was progressing with many of the Sunday journalists present too, but it was also great to see people like Rob Wildman, Neil Squires and Paul Stephens, as they had been there at the start of Brian Kennedy's reign at the club.

The photo shoot was an incredible exercise with forty-six photographers present, all wanting team shots as well as head and shoulder photos of the whole squad. The Sharks players have always been a pleasure to deal with and we had designed a chart to show where players had to stand to make the team photo look more professional. The photographers took their photos as Jason sat on the left of the front row, the position he always liked to sit in until he became captain, and all the players seated at the front had been briefed to clean their boots. The cameras started clicking off and the television crews were working around the edges too, filming for their bulletins. The great thing about the 2002 shoot was that we had entered the digital age and I was able to look at the photos before letting the players go. The previous year Jim Bramhall and Adam Black had done the old trick of putting a hand on each other's knee, which infuriated co-owner Ian Blackhurst when his company paid for 10,000 posters and postcards to be printed.

Alphabetical order is always the best way of taking head and shoulders shots, but it is amazing how many players don't know that D follows C and T follows the letter S!

The head and shoulder shots seemed to be taking an age and my son Dan was ticking the players off on his chart before shouting, "Robbo, where are you?"

We looked around towards the chairs set up for the team shot to see Robbo had fallen asleep! Club photographer Clint Hughes snapped Robbo in the land of nod. Jason's wife Amanda was expecting their third child so he was helping out where he could around the house and with the children. Earlier in the day he had asked me to contact Santus in Wigan, who make Uncle Joe's Mint Balls, a Northern delicacy, because Amanda had a craving for them. I rang the Winnard brothers who own Santus, and they donated a jar of the sweets with their compliments.

During the close season Dan had an idea for a Media v Players Sevens competition and Jim Mallinder, Jos Baxendell, Apollo Perelini and Robbo took part. Steve Diamond said he would only take part if the outgoing Chief Executive Carl Fox was playing and that he wanted to be on the opposite team – I can't think why!

James Cooper, then a Granada Reports sports reporter, took part and in the first minutes of the game he tried to sell Robbo a dummy and collided with Jason's forearm! It was like a move from Sky Sports Wrestling and had Apollo asking Jason for lessons in the art of 'clotheslining' an opponent. The game saw Jim Mallinder showing many of the moves that had made him a Sale legend before Jason attacked down the right, drew the defender and sent my son Dan in for the only try of the game.

On Granada television that evening James Cooper showed Jason's 'tackle' and then ran it again in slow motion. In the after-match interview Jason said that he thought James had taken a dive! Dan was so proud that he had scored the winner and was 'made up' when the try was shown on Granada.

Season tickets had sold well in the close season after the success of the previous season, and we all looked forward to the new campaign.

We played Borders in a pre-season warm-up game and blew them away before lining up against Northampton Saints on the opening day of the season. A crowd of 5,313 packed into the ground to see the Sharks grind out a 24-21 win. Ben Cohen scored a try early in the game and Sale Sharks' only points came from the boot. Charlie Hodgson kicked six penalties and a drop goal while long-serving Jos Baxendell chipped in with a match-winning drop goal. After the game, Jim Mallinder said that he thought the performance was very professional and that the tries that had been scored so freely the previous season would return.

Octagon, Jason's representation, had organised some fixture cards for the club with Jason's picture on the other side. Dan had organised Jason to sign two hundred for the young fans and these were distributed so that he could get some food with the rest of his team-mates. I organised the Press Conference and then met up with Robbo who was dining with Charlie Hodgson and Mark Cueto.

"Swanny, when I have finished do you fancy a walk on the pitch, I want to show you something," he said.

"Go on then, but hurry up, I want to get home to bed," I replied.

We walked the full length of the Heywood Road pitch and stood at the top end.

"See that tree there, can you organise it to be cut back? I can't see the ball when it is hoisted high and don't want to have to wait until the Autumn before I can catch the ball," he smiled.

"Do my best Robbo, anything else while I am here?" I said

smilingly.

"Well make sure the club don't put brighter bulbs in the floodlights, that's my secret weapon. I get the ball and run at the defence and I am in full flight before they can see me, it gives me a big advantage!" he laughed.

The following week Sale Sharks visited Gloucester, who many had tipped for the title. Sale Sharks lost 44–8 and Brian Kennedy was so disappointed that he had walked out on the whistle to go home. Brian is such a passionate fan as well as benefactor to the club that heavy defeats hurt him.

Leicester Tigers were next on the agenda at Heywood Road, having beaten Harlequins the week before. Full house notices were posted the day before the game and we all hoped for a quick recovery after the Gloucester defeat. The players always used to have a pre-match meeting in one of the bar areas and as Robbo was passing me pitchside, I said, "Sorted it Robbo, floodlights are more powerful and the tree has been left as you wanted." This was my way of paying him back for all the jokes I had been on the receiving end of. Robbo halted for a minute and said, "If you have done that Swanny, I am bringing some ladders next week to chop the trees back and take some bulbs out."

The game was a classic and the Sharks ran out 29–16 winners. Bryan Redpath scored an early try but had to leave the field shortly afterwards, seeing stars following a high shot. Second-rower Chris Jones sprinted 50 metres leaving defenders in his slipstream to score the try of the evening. Robbo said that he thought Jonesy resembled an Emu in full flight, but he was proud of his team-mate's incredible try. Wins against Harlequins and London Irish followed as well as a high-scoring draw at Leeds Tykes but the most notable thing was that Robbo's tries had dried up again. Bourgoin visited Heywood Road in the first pool game of the Heineken Cup early in October and there was needle before the kick-off as Bourgoin had alleged that Sale Sharks had spied on their training session at a nearby college. Bourgoin's Director of Rugby was Philippe Saint Andre, and he had dragged the French team out of the gutter to make them a European force to be reckoned with. Jason scored his first try of the season and the lead was changing hands regularly in the pouring rain. A brass band played throughout the game to build the atmosphere and there were some mixed feelings about this from supporters.

Just before the break the Bourgoin backrow player, one Sebastien Chabal - now a Sharks hero - launched himself at Jason and left him face down in the mud. Robbo was hurt and had to have a dressing applied and he was limping when he returned for the second half. Chabal had done a job on Jason but worse was yet to come. Following a mistake in midfield, a Bourgoin player kicked ahead and Jason was running neck and neck with a huge Bourgoin forward. There was some shirt pulling before the Bourgoin player fell over. Now we are talking about a five feet eight inch player against one six foot plus and the weight advantage was about six stones in the French player's favour. The referee amazingly gave a penalty try and sinbinned Jason, who hobbled off to the dressing room.

Sale Sharks lost the game and Steve Diamond lost his temper with the Welsh referee. Bourgoin had used their front row substitutes and the referee allowed uncontested scrums for the last fifteen minutes. I could see Steve making his way towards the official shouting abuse at him. I tried to calm Steve down but he had lost it. I gave the players ten minutes to chill out before making an entry into the dressing room to take Jim Mallinder to the Press Conference. Jim, a gentleman, was composed and paid tribute to the players who had given everything, not once querying the referee's decisions. After the journalists had finished quizzing him, we left and

Mally asked me to get the match commissioner for him, as he wanted to check out a few things. The problem was that Sale Sharks had gone up another level to the Heineken Cup and Philippe Saint Andre and his troops were more street-wise. Jim and Steve were excellent young coaches and had been outstanding the previous season, but this was the big league and they both knew they had some learning to do. Jim has since gone on to join the England Academy set-up while Dimes is now Head Coach at Saracens. Both were great to work with but you always had to be on your guard with Dimes as he had a great sense of humour but could turn on you quickly. I was on the wrong end of Dimes' temper a few times but he never held grudges and once he had said his piece it was forgotten.

The week after the Bourgoin defeat, Graeme Bond arrived from Australia. Graeme had played for the Brumbies as well as Australia and was an incredible talent with an equally in-credible haircut. He said he had grown his locks to protect himself from the Manchester winter that was just around the corner. Graeme was a class player and a great bloke too. He was hoping to acclimatise before making his debut, but that went out of the window in his first week. Jason's wife Amanda was expecting their third child so he drove up to Glasgow in his car with the intention of driving straight back after the final whistle. Graeme had gone for the ride but shortly before kick off Jason got the call that the birth of his child was imminent. Jim Mallinder allowed him to drive home while giving Graeme Bond his debut on a freezing cold night in Glasgow. Robbo arrived back in Lancashire just after Joseph was born and rang me the following day with the weigh-in details.

As Sale Sharks had two away games together, Carole and I jetted out to Dubai for some sun and sightseeing.

As we prepared to board the plane I received a text message

from Robbo telling me to have a good rest and to haggle with the 'Looky Looky' man!

Suffice to say you don't find 'Looky Looky' men in Dubai and there is very little street crime as the majority of the locals are wealthier than I will ever be.

On the day we came home we were making good time until we crossed the North Sea where the wind was incredible. Emirates Airlines have screens in the back of the seats and you are able to watch the plane descend and land. As we approached the runway, the screen showed grass, tarmac, grass then grass, grass, tarmac and grass. I must admit I said one to Robbo's mate upstairs and was so relieved when the wheels hit the tarmac.

When I arrived home I found out that Sale Sharks had lost at Newcastle before realising that Robbo was scheduled to fly from Newcastle to join up with the England squad for the Autumn international training session. I rang Robbo who said, "You would not believe the flight I have just had, Swanny, seat belts on all the way and worst of all they didn't serve any refreshments on the flight."

Here is Robbo more upset about the lack of snacks rather than flying in a force ten gale! Sometimes I just shake my head and wonder whether anything would ever faze him.

November 2002 will be remembered as the month when England took on the best and beat them with style. First up at Twickenham were New Zealand, who were beaten 31-28. In this game Jason came up against Jonah Lomu for the first time and told me that he was the most difficult player he had ever tried to tackle. Give Robbo his due, though, he slowed the Kiwi giant down! The following week I sat down in the flat to watch the game against Australia when my mobile went off. It was the police asking me to go to Jason's home to sort out the alarm. Great, I thought, Robbo is taking on the Aussies and I am in the car listening to the radio in between the football commentary. I sorted out the problem and, as I was driving back to Lytham, listened to the post-match interviews after England had beaten the Aussies 32-31.

The following week was like watching a Wigan v Warrington match in the eighties, spiteful from the first whistle to last. The tactics of the Springboks were nothing short of disgraceful and after Jonny Wilkinson had been flattened, Jason was kicked in the side of the head when he was stood up at the time! The result was that Robbo received a perforated eardrum. England, led superbly by Martin Johnson, trounced the Springboks 53-3. Johnno was targeted but never once reacted or retaliated and he proved he is and will be for a long time an England legend.

Robbo returned back home and Sale Sharks Club Doctors Dave Jones and Geraint Allen organised an x-ray for Jason's head. Jason, though, had other ideas and wanted to play for Sale Sharks the following week against Bath with an earful of cotton wool protecting his injury. Sharks won the game 36-18 in front of a capacity crowd. Everything went well and Robbo was given some medication by the Doctor before going home. The following day I checked in with Robbo to see if he was okay and to tell him I had three journalists chasing him for an interview.

"Swanny, hold off on the interviews, it's been an incredible six weeks with Joseph being born and the three England games," he said.

"How's your ear?" I asked.

"Swanny, you would not believe what I did, I was in the bath and lay back and submerged my head, the water ran into my ear and I leapt out of the bath in agony. It's the worst pain I have ever had," he said.

"Did the water run down your nose from your perforated eardrum?" I joked, remembering the lack of sympathy I got when he hurt my fingers the year before.

"Thanks pal," he laughed.

I had numerous calls from Malcolm Folley who was moving on at speed with Jason's book. Malcolm lived in the south and travelled up regularly to spend time with Jason as *Finding My Feet* took shape.

The first week of December we played Llanelli at Heywood Road in the Heineken Cup and again the 'house full' signs were posted early. The game will be remembered for a big fight between the players in the first half to which the referee reacted in a strange way. He missed the start of the fight so he sent off the last two players fighting on the floor! Sharks lost 30-19 and, to cap it all, the club was raided in the early hours of the morning and the bar takings were stolen. If things could not get any worse I picked up a speeding ticket on the way home for doing 34 in a 30 mph zone.

The following week the team played the return match in Llanelli. Sharks had lost their first three in the Heineken Cup, so qualification for the latter stages had disappeared out of the window. Jim Mallinder was struggling for players in South Wales and named the only twenty-two players he had available. Jim also asked Jason to captain the team. Robbo agreed and was looking forward to his new, albeit temporary role. The players travelled down on the day to keep costs down and as we were having some work done at home I took Bazil the Lhasa Apso with me to work as I was having an early finish. Robbo took one look at Bazil and then proceeded to tell the players that my pet dog was a monster! The players made a fuss of Bazil but Robbo came nowhere near his little foe.

The game was lost 17-12 but Jim Mallinder told me that all the players had given their all and that Jason was an inspiration from full back as acting captain.

The following week we were dumped out of the Powergen Cup at Saracens after being demolished in the first half. The

Christmas game was lost at Bristol and Robbo told me the weather was the worst he had ever experienced – this changed during the following season.

Newcastle Falcons were the first visitors to Heywood Road in January 2003 on a freezing cold Friday evening. Sale Sharks tore Newcastle apart, scoring five tries including a Jason special. Ever since Rob Andrew had upped the stakes in 2001 with his Albania comments, games between the two clubs at Heywood Road have become 'must win' fixtures. Sadly, Jonny Wilkinson did not play in the game as he was recovering from injury at the time.

At the end of the month Sale Sharks travelled to Knowsley Road, the home of St Helens Rugby League Club, for a cross-code challenge that I had discussed with then coach Ian Millward a few months earlier. Ian is an effervescent character who loves the game of Rugby League and wanted a chance of taking on a Rugby Union side. We knocked the idea about between us, and then the Sharks' Chief Executive Niels de Vos and the St Helens Chairman got together and thrashed out the logistics. The concept was unique, one half Rugby League and one half Rugby Union, but the points scoring structure would be the same throughout the game as the higher points value of Rugby Union would have created an imbalance. Scrums were to be uncontested as the heavier Rugby Union forwards could have injured the Saints and the tackling technique of Rugby League of hitting across the chest was toned down. It was agreed that the game would be played, Rugby Union for the first half and Rugby League for the second. Amazingly, a crowd of over 12,000 turned up on a horrible night when it rained and there was a strong wind. Coronation Street had a strong storyline at the time too; the main attraction, though, was Jason Robinson back on a Rugby League field. Brian Kennedy had sought clearance for Jason, as he was due to be training with England to prepare for the Six Nations.

I arrived early for the game and met up with Jason who had left his car at Apollo Perelini's house so that he could drive to Manchester Airport the following morning to catch the plane to London.

Walking around the pitch with Apollo, Jason said that nothing had changed. The Saints fans booed him as they always did, but they also called him a traitor for moving to Rugby Union. There were even a number of Wigan fans on the ground cheering on St Helens, which is unheard of as the two clubs are archenemies!

In the first half Sharks rattled up 41 points and St Helens failed to score. At half time the St Helens announcer made a fool of himself ripping the game of Rugby Union to pieces with childish comments, but we just sat in the directors box, tight lipped, wondering whether we could hold St Helens out, to win the game.

St Helens started the second half like a house on fire and rattled up points at the rate of one a minute, but the young Sharks players played man-to-man marking and it was all getting very tense towards the end of the game. At 41-39, Sean Long had the chance to tie the scores but fluffed his conversion and the hooter sounded. The St Helens' coaching team demanded more time but Steve Diamond told the Sharks players that was it, we had won and added that as Sharks did not have a timekeeper, the man blowing the hooter in the stand was in fact a St Helens employee.

I spoke to Robbo after the game and said, "I thought you were only going to do an hour."

He replied, "Swanny, once a Wiganer always a Wiganer and when you are in front against them, you would play on with two broken legs!" It was a shame that some of the Wigan fans in the crowd chose to boo and heckle their former hero.

The Press Conference was incredible in that Ian Millward said Union was boring while Jim Mallinder paid tribute to the skills of the St Helens players. As I said previously, Ian is passionate about Rugby League and I think the defeat had hurt him.

In the players' bar afterwards the mood was strange. The Sharks players were buoyant and the Saints players were really down. Steve Smith, a former Sale player who is now a Director, upset the apple cart when he came in beaming and said, "It's taken 108 years and Union is still the superior sport," referring of course to the Union - League split in 1895.

I sent a text message to Peter Deakin, telling him that we had won, as I know he would have been proud of the lads that evening.

The newspapers the following day hailed the Sharks win but one or two of the papers were rude towards us. Robbo told me not to react badly as I wanted to pick up the phone and give some media men I had previously respected both barrels.

The Rugby League website had a swipe at Ian Millward saying he had betrayed Rugby League, and it was quite amusing as the week wore on that people could respond so childishly over a game. I received letters from St Helens fans that we circulated round the staff. They were bizarre in that they were so bitter they were laughable. The whole exercise was to put on a show and give both clubs' coffers a boost. While the St Helens fans were penning venomous letters and posting obscene messages on websites, I was helping Saints plan their travel route to the South of France for a Challenge Cup tie!

The Sale Sharks fans were pleased with the win but, to be honest, were not really bothered about the result. We did have a laugh at the video that was made on the evening as it featured a very one-sided commentary. We sold about five hundred videos of the game and people bought them mainly for the commentary!

Holiday time had come around again and at the end of January Carole and I packed up ready to go to Jamaica. Robbo asked me to bring him back a dreadlock hat and some jerk chicken spread for his barbecue. The day before I finished work, I took a phone call from Deaks who said he had quit at Saracens and was going back to live in Warrington. He said he wanted to take a 'time out' and recover his health. Deaks joked about me going to Jamaica and said that when I returned home I had to ring him to organise a get together, and that I should bring Jason and Apollo with me.

When Carole and I arrived at our hotel in Montego Bay, we had a message to ring home and being 5,000-plus miles away from home you always fear the worst. Carole's daughter Emma told me that Deaks had died earlier that day. I tried to ring Peter's wife Michelle without success and I was in a state of shock. Deaks had taken me to Warrington Wolves and then to Sale Sharks and had played a huge part in my career. I contacted my son Dan, who did a sterling job organising a card and some flowers and was able to get in touch with both Jason and Apollo to tell them the sad news and ask them if they were going to the funeral. Needless to say, Jason was there to pay his respects alongside Apollo. Jason liked Deaks and paid tribute to him in his autobiography.

Newspapers are difficult to obtain in the Caribbean but I will always remember buying the *Daily Mail* and reading Peter Jackson's tribute piece to Deaks. The day of the funeral was two days before we returned home but working out the time difference I sat in the chapel and said one for Peter. It was the first time I had cried in a long time, but Deaks meant a lot to me and had laid some crucial foundations in the success of Bradford Bulls, Warrington Wolves and Sale Sharks.

During my holiday the Sharks won at both London Irish and Harlequins.

When I returned home the Six Nations were about to start. England started well with a win over France followed by a 26-9 win over Wales under the closed roof of the Millennium Stadium in Cardiff. Robbo pulled a muscle in the first half and had to be replaced by Phil Christophers. The muscle injury improved after two weeks' treatment but it was an injury that can still give Jason problems today. He missed the win against Italy but was determined to play for Sale Sharks in the televised Premiership clash against Leeds Tykes. In the Italy game, young Sale Sharks fly half Charlie Hodgson suffered a horrific knee injury when his studs caught in the turf and the Sharks hunt for a top three finish started to disintegrate.

In the week running up to the Leeds game Jason received a letter from a young fan who lived in Lincolnshire and the thread of the letter said that Jason had better watch out, as this youngster wanted his place in the England team. I showed Robbo the letter and he said, "How old is he?"

"Eight," I replied.

"Tell you what Swanny, invite him and his family to the Leeds game as my guest as I want to meet this little lad with big ambitions," Robbo said.

I wrote to Matthew and asked him to pass the letter to his parents who contacted me and we set everything up for him and his family to watch the game and meet him after the match.

On the day of the game I met Matthew and while we were chatting outside the club shop, Robbo ran round the corner, late for the team meeting after physio on his muscle injury. When Robbo spotted Matthew he slammed on the brakes and said, "You must be Matthew who wants my place in the England team, I hope you are good." The look on Matthew's face was priceless and I am sure he will remember it for a long time to come.

Robbo turned on the style during the game and scored two tries, one of which was one of the best he had ever scored in either code. Graeme Bond offloaded on the half-way line and Robbo jinked right then left and turned on the gas to score what Sky commentator Miles Harrison called a sensational try.

Clint Hughes, the club photographer, snapped the try on a sequence of photos and at one stage there were seven players chasing Robbo. I asked Clint to take some photos after the game of Jason presenting some of his playing kit to young Matthew Doyley.

Ever since Matthew's visit we have invited several of Jason's fans to games to meet him. We have had fans from as far away as Scotland, Cornwall and Kent coming to meet Jason who spends time chatting with them. Jason selects the letters, which I have to shortlist for him because, believe it or not, Robbo receives over a hundred letters a week.

Jason returned to the England team for the Calcutta Cup game against Scotland at Twickenham and it was a game of mixed emotions for him, scoring two tries but being sin-binned for body checking Kenny Logan. I rang Robbo in the evening after the game and said he was becoming cynical in his old age, having being sin-binned twice in the last six months! Robbo was not best pleased with Kenny though – he thought he had made a three-course meal out of the collision. England went on to win the Six Nations Grand Slam in Ireland with a 42-6 win at Lansdowne Road.

Heywood Road was at bursting point during the 2002-2003 season and rumours circulated that Brian Kennedy was looking to move the Sharks away from Sale. Several grounds were looked at including Maine Road, shortly to be vacated by Manchester City, Lancashire County Cricket Club and several sites in the Sale area. The local council did not seem interested in getting involved and it came as no surprise that Brian bought Edgeley Park, home to Stockport County. Stockport was ten miles from Heywood Road and while there were rumblings from a section of fans the move proved to be a shrewd one in the long term.

Gloucester visited Heywood Road on Good Friday and shared in a 30-30 draw in which Robbo turned in a five-star performance, scoring an incredible try when he looked to have been closed down by the Gloucester defence. Steve Hanley and Mark Cueto also scored tries as the Sale Sharks potent back three came up trumps again.

Steve Hanley has been with the club since 1998 but Mark Cueto only really broke through at the start of Jason's first full season. Mark has watched Jason closely and uses him as a role model to great effect. He regularly pays tribute to Jason and they are good friends off the field. Mark, like Jason, is a great PR role model who is well respected by the fans and the media because he is always available for interview.

The last game at Heywood Road was against London Wasps which Sale Sharks lost 16-9. It was not the best way to finish at the old ground but the rain poured down, supporters were soaked and Wasps skipper Lawrence Dallaglio was inspirational in his leadership. The players were down at the final whistle although they had finished fourth and had qualified for the Heineken Cup again. When the players had changed I sat with Jason and Bryan Redpath in the players' dining room. After a short while Jason started laughing and couldn't stop.

Bryan said, "What's up wee man?"

Robbo regained his composure and said, "Bryan, you're a great player and a rugged little character but picking a fight with Lawrence Dallaglio, who is about two foot bigger than you, was hilarious."

Jason and Bryan became big friends on day one and Robbo, ever the joker, reckons that Bryan is the only player he has ever played with who is smaller than him. Bryan always laughs it off, but then again he has to. The first wisecrack Jason made about Bryan was back in 2001 when we used to have posters to advertise games drawn for display in pubs, schools and shops. I had the idea to put Jason and Bryan on the same poster as they were current internationals, but Robbo said, "Swanny, when you ask the cartoonist to draw it, make sure that I am a lot taller than Brush [Bryan's nickname]." I did as Robbo asked and when Bryan saw it he gave me a volley of Celtic curses, laughing as he blasted me.

I was still hurting after Peter Deakin's death and wanted him to be remembered within the game. I came up with the idea of the 'Man of the Match' award in the Premiership Final being named after Deaks. I floated the idea with the better-known rugby writers, lobbying for support, and then wrote to Premier Rugby's Chief Executive Howard Thomas. The award was introduced but I was surprised that I learned about it in a newspaper as I thought Howard Thomas, a former Chief Executive at Sale, might have acknowledged my letter. Still you live and learn, but several of the game's top writers rang me to thank me for my efforts and said they knew where the idea had originated. The best part of the Peter Deakin Award was that his widow Michelle and young son Theo were invited to Twickenham to present it. I told Robbo about the Peter Deakin Award and said it would be nice if he were to win it before he retired. Robbo had won every award available in Rugby League and several in Rugby Union but is ever the team man.

During the close season Robbo jetted off down under to play for England in World Cup warm-up games against Australia and New Zealand. Both games were won and England rugby fans began to believe that it might be

England's destiny to win in Australia in the autumn.

We had to work some of the week at Heywood Road and also spend some time at Edgeley Park, preparing for the ground move. One of the first visitors was Jason along with his son Cameron. Robbo was easily recognisable, even to football fans and the people of Stockport soon accepted him.

My son Dan decided to leave during the close season, as he wanted a better-paid job and everyone at the club, including the players, were sad to see him leave. The coaching and office staff and the players bought him cards and presents and Robbo took Dan out for a meal before dropping him off at home in Abbey Village just outside Chorley. Dan told me that when Jason's Land Rover pulled up outside his house it turned a few heads in the street and his credibility rating was sky high.

The autobiography went to print and one day a lorry arrived with three pallets full of books. I thought, great, a sneak preview of it but Robbo was adamant that I would have to wait until nearer publication date. Robbo wasn't being nasty, but he wanted me to see what he had written about me when I was relaxed and away from the club.

I was sent a copy of Jason's book by Sian Masterton of Octagon and put it in my brief case. When I read it I was very flattered to be referred to as 'my right hand man' by Jason and was delighted he gave Dan a few mentions too. Dan still dines out on the book and still keeps in touch with Robbo on a regular basis. Jason is always giving him advice and sees a lot of himself in Dan, who has settled down a lot from his early days at Heywood Road but the banter between Jason and Dan is very funny when they meet up at Sharks home games.

The Press day was organised and I asked Robbo if he was attending even though he was due to meet up with England in readiness for the World Cup.

"Course I am coming, I haven't missed one of your Press days yet, have I? Line the interviews up in fifteen minute intervals and let's get them done quickly," Robbo said.

"That should be easy then, there are only two requests to speak to you," I said.

"Must be losing my popularity then, never mind," he replied.

"Don't be daft, there are twenty-one requests to speak to you face-to-face and two phoners, plus one who wants to interview you by text message," I said with a smile as I could not resist the chance to get one over on him.

We had the Press photographs in the sun and Jason did some interviews sitting on the Edgeley Park turf before retiring to the Pavilion Suite to start his interviews.

Some journalists have a habit of spending the first fifteen minutes of interviews telling Jason what they have done and I have worked on this over the years by explaining to the culprits that Robbo's time is tight and they should explain pleasantries before going straight into question one.

Jason always prefers one-to-one interviews and sometimes he must get a little jaded when the same questions are asked over and over again.

Reading the newspapers over the years the stories have been done to death about Jason's younger years, his drinking, wild lifestyle and turning to Christianity. They are all stories to be told but in writing this book I wanted to show *The Real Jason Robinson* and how he is as a human being. The mail he receives is incredible and the demands on his time numerous.

On the day of the Press Conference I received an e-mail from a man in Tokyo asking Jason if he would fly to Japan en route to the World Cup to give his testimony in a ten-minute presentation! Suffice to say, Jason did not make an appearance.

Jason sees only a small proportion of the mail sent to him at the club and that is the way we have worked it over the years. Some of the letters are quite upsetting, some include racial abuse, some from Rugby League fans who are still annoyed he left to join Sale Sharks but mainly they are requests for autographs and are complimentary. The amazing ones are those from, for example, a boy scouts' group in Cornwall asking if Jason will travel down on a Wednesday night to present awards and they usually finish with "it will only take half an hour!" Now I was good at Geography at school and know that it's unrealistic to make a 500 miles-plus mile return trip for a half hour appearance.

With the book launch imminent I had a phone call from an old friend in Wigan, Trevor Smith. Trevor owns a bookshop, Smith's of Wigan and wanted to know about the possibility of Robbo doing a signing session.

Robbo said, "Do you think it's a good idea, Swanny? I mean some of the Wigan fans are still upset I left."

"Robbo, you are well loved in Wigan and I am sure Trevor will look after you," I replied.

"Go on then, but ask him to get me a tuna and sweetcorn sandwich for my dinner and can you ask your lass [Carole] if I can park on the hotel car park where she works? I don't want to get a ticket or worse still clamped," he said.

"Sorted, now go and enjoy yourself at Trevor's," I finished.

Trevor sold out of books, having ordered 500 and Robbo signed them all as well as enjoying the company of some of the Wigan fans who had fond memories of his time at the club.

Robbo arrived at Edgeley Park late in the afternoon and did another signing session in the club shop when another 500 books were sold to Sharks fans.

That evening Sale Sharks played Northampton Saints in the opening game of the season in front of a new club record attendance, in excess of 8,000. Jason did not play in the game, which ended 37-37. Robbo joked at half time, "Swanny, get me my boots, I could improve my try-scoring record tonight!" Sadly he could not take part as he was under wraps for the World Cup and the plane would leave for Australia within days.

WORLD CUP TRIUMPH

The 2003-2004 season began poorly for Sale Sharks following the move to Edgeley Park. The main factors were the new surroundings for the players as well as absentees due to the forthcoming World Cup competition down under.

I kept in touch with Jason on a daily basis while he was in Australia. Robbo likes his creature comforts and hates being away from his family and his home. Amanda travelled over after a few weeks but the rigours of training, team meetings and games meant that he was seeing very little of his family. Jason is very protective about his family and I have lost count over the years the number of offers of money for an "At home with the Robinsons." Apart from anything else Jason believes it is an open invitation to potential burglars to 'case the joint' if you are sat there at home, photographed with the family. I can see his point really.

Another no-go area is being a panellist on *A Question of Sport*. Not that Jason has anything against the BBC; it's just that he does not feel confident of his knowledge of sport to do the programme justice.

We did do the mystery guest for *A Question of Sport* though. After much persuasion, Jason agreed to pose as Dooley Wilson the pianist in Casablanca and said he would do it if I would help. Robbo played the piano badly - it's amazing how they made it sound on air - while I was sitting having a drink at the bar. We were both in tuxedos and well paid for one hour's work. I got the full equity rate and Robbo reckoned his fee would keep us both in lunches for a few weeks.

Amazing, I have known Jason all these years and we rarely speak about money - it's not important. He does have a go sometimes, jokingly, saying that he was the makeweight in the deal that brought me to Sale Sharks and his classic was that he reckoned if I won the lottery it would be a tax inconvenience. The usual reply is, "In your dreams, pal!"

I was able to update Jason with Charlie Hodgson's progress after his bad knee injury, which had cost Charlie a World Cup squad place with England.

Sale Sharks' first victory of the season came at Welford Road in October with a 22-16 win over Leicester Tigers, the first time Sale had won there. I sent Jason a text after the game and he was delighted and put in calls to the coaches and playing staff the following day.

The following Friday was the eve of the World Cup, and Wasps beat Sale Sharks 37-33. I held off the text messages and waited for Jason's promised call after the opening game against Georgia in Perth. He was upbeat and was satisfied with his performance but thought the team performance needed to improve.

The next England game was against South Africa, again at the Subiaco Oval in Perth. It was the first time the teams had met since the ugly game at Twickenham the previous Autumn. Fifty thousand packed into the stadium and it took England a while to break down the Springboks, but a Will Greenwood try kick-started England and together with twenty Jonny Wilkinson points the Springboks were beaten 25-6.

Sale Sharks were starting to get their season on track with successive wins at Harlequins and Rotherham and England had seen off their biggest group threat in South Africa. Winning the World Cup was now a strong possibility.

I rang Jason the evening before the Samoan game and he was upbeat and glad to hear from me. I was able to fill him in with all the events from the club and tell him his book was selling well. He joked, "Has anyone recognised you from the picture in the book yet, Swanny?"

"No mate, I have had my hair done differently," I replied.

The laughing at the other end of the phone was great to hear. I am bald and it's a big joke between us, especially when I point out that he is going grey and will look like Lenny Henry's character Donovan Bogard before he is forty.

"I shouldn't laugh Swanny but the other day Geoff Green was at the Press Conference and you know he wears a wig? It was so hot that he came to the conference without it and I just cracked up," Robbo said.

Geoff is proud of his hairpiece and been on the end of jokes, I believe for years, but this must have been a rare occasion where he did not wear it.

We chatted for about ten minutes before we called it a day and he thanked me for my call.

The following day was a real eye opener as England struggled to break the Samoans down until the latter stages, running out 35-22 winners. The big problem was that the whole England squad had been relocated to Melbourne from Perth, which in old money is a long way!

After this game, it was all move again up the East coast to Brisbane and the final group game against Uruguay. Robbo told me he was benched for this game and he was hoping to sit it out. The best-laid plans go wrong though and four minutes after half time, Robbo replaced Iain Balshaw. He scored two tries in his thirty-six minute run out as England won 111-13.

Sale Sharks were blowing hot and cold, losing at home to London Irish before winning against Leeds Tykes. Charlie Hodgson made his long-awaited comeback in this game and Robbo rang Charlie the night before the game for a chat. Charlie had had a roller coaster career with Sale Sharks in that he was breaking into the first team when Jason arrived, had a record breaking England debut and had then been hit with two serious knee injuries costing him a trip Down Under. Charlie is an incredibly talented player and his time will come. He works so hard, day in day out and it's a shame that he is constantly compared to Jonny Wilkinson. Then again, if you were asked to name the 1966 England World Cup winners the majority would say Geoff Hurst first of all before naming the other ten.

I rang Jason after the Leeds game and told him we had won 37-21 with a bonus point. He said, "How did Charlie go?" I told him he had done well and Robbo said, "37-21 and a bonus point, do you think I will get back in the team?"

The following day England stuttered against Wales before winning 28-17. Most alarming was that Wales scored three tries to England's one and many thought the England boys would be home in time to watch the final on television!

On the weekend of the semi-finals, Sale Sharks had to travel to Leicester Tigers in the Powergen Cup. Visiting Welford Road once a season is enough but this was the Sharks' second trip to the Tigers in six weeks. The majority of the media were in Australia, but those left behind believed Sharks would be well beaten. It was great to ring Jason in his hotel room in Sydney to leave him a wake up message that we had won 43-28 in extra time and that we would be at home to Saracens in the quarter-final in the new year.

"Just think Robbo, we might even win this competition when you return! Now go and sort out the Frogs," was the message he would receive when he awoke on the morning of the game.

The semi-final against France was never going to be a classic and the England try-scoring machine seemed to have dried up. Jonny Wilkinson kicked all the England points with five penalties and three-drop goals. England had made the final and had hardly hit top form. Clive Woodward was cautious in his post-match press conference but it did not take an expert to read into Martin Johnson's comments to realise that England needed to step up their performance in the final.

The week running up to the game went so quickly. Sale Sharks had a home game on the eve of the final against Saracens. Everything was in place from my department, ready to enjoy the game - that was until I got a phonecall from a journalist with some shocking information.

I will not reveal the source but he said, "Swanny, you are not going to believe this but one of the Sunday tabloids are planning to dig the dirt on Robbo, win or lose, and one of them has been 'doorstepping' Jason's family."

The first thing I did was make a cup of coffee, then light a cigarette. Where Robbo uses fast food for fuel, I use caffeine and tobacco. I made a call to Sian Masterton and Clifford Bloxham at Octagon who started to make calls to the newspaper concerned and the mobile phones, landlines and emails were overheating, as was my anger!

The journalist doing the doorstepping was very persistent until he was approached by one of Jason's former Wigan team-mates who persuaded the 'journalist' it would be in his own interest to go home. A sickening and thankfully minority of journalists amaze me in that after a sports star peaks they feel it their responsibility to discredit them. Everything about Jason's past had been written in Finding my Feet but here was a paper offering money for a story. I cannot name the paper for legal reasons but it is not hard to work out which one of the Sundays Jason never speaks to!

Meanwhile Robbo knew nothing about this, or so we thought. Sale Sharks smashed Saracens 33-3 and as I had done throughout the World Cup, I sent a text message to Jason with the result and to wish him all the best for the following day. You never say 'good luck' to Robbo, as he does not believe in 'luck'.

I woke early on the day of the final and put in a call to Richard Prescott, who is Director of Communications for the Rugby Union and a good friend.

I told Richard about the newspaper and asked his advice. Richard replied, "Swanny, Jason is aware of what has been going on and is very angry."

I asked Richard, "Is Robbo okay and up for the game?"

Richard replied, "Swanny, he is well up for this, but win or lose, he is refusing to speak to the press after the game. I rang around the nationals after Robbo told me and they were very understanding about the situation but annoyed at the paper concerned."

The game was a blur; I remember Jason being out-jumped by Tuqiri for a try not dissimilar to the one in the 1998 cup final and then scoring from a move involving Lawrence Dallaglio and Jonny Wilkinson."

Extra time seemed to take an age, and then I remember punching the air forgetting Bazil, my pet dog, was on my knee at the time when Jonny's drop goal sailed between the posts!

Carole and I were due to go to Las Vegas the following week for a break and had to pick up our travellers' cheques from the bank in Wigan. Before we dashed to Wigan I remember seeing the post-match interviews, but no Jason. He had meant what he said to Richard Prescott.

In Wigan about an hour later, I had just signed my final travellers' cheque when the mobile phone rang. It was Robbo and his mood was subdued rather then ecstatic.

"Swanny, when I come home I don't want any journalist from that paper anywhere near me."

I said, " Is that why you punched the ball into Row Z when you scored?" I thought trying to make light of the situation might help. Jason said that his emotions were mixed at that time, elation through scoring a try and annoyed about the previous day's developments.

"Jason, why not do a few interviews, you have helped shape history for the game?"

He replied, "No chance, I have bent over backwards for newspapers and to do that to me is totally lacking in respect."

I told him that one of his former team-mates had persuaded the journalist to go home, but Robbo said that the whole situation should not have happened.

I believe he was more upset than annoyed and it was a side of Jason I had never experienced. He felt betrayed more than anything with the lack of respect he had been afforded.

We chatted for about five minutes before he said goodbye as he had to attend a post-match meal. But within a short space of time, I was taking calls from the media from both sides of the world, asking which paper had been to blame for Jason's non-appearance at the post-match press conference.

I didn't envy Richard Prescott having to deal with the 'no-show Jason' who had scored the only England try, but Richard is a professional who took it in his stride, just as he did when England had had sixteen players on the field for thirty seconds earlier in the tournament.

I must admit it was very tempting to 'name and shame' the paper concerned but I didn't have to worry too long as the journalists guessed the name of the publication. I was upset for two of the journalists who worked for the paper as I had a good working relationship with them and hoped that time would be a great healer.

The day after the game Robbo did a great PR exercise for Sale Sharks in that he posed with the William Webb Ellis Trophy on the beach wearing his Sale Sharks jersey. The club sponsors AMD and Cotton Traders were naturally delighted.

I bought all the papers to cut the match reports out and the paper that had wanted to cause havoc 'dealing the dirt' was sycophantic to a nauseating degree. I saved the Press Cuttings in a file to give to Robbo on his return home.

On the Sunday evening Robbo called me and asked me to do him a favour. He was flying in on the newly-named 'Sweet Chariot' aeroplane and was catching the internal flight back up to Manchester.

"I am due in early and am coming straight back North. Can you pick me up from Terminal Three and can you ring my car sponsor and ask them to deliver my car to Edgeley Park."

"No problem, I will be circling Manchester Airport at 8am, ring me on the mobile and I will come and get you," I replied.

The television stations showed the plane landing and the thousands of people at the airport wanting to cheer their heroes. No Robbo though, he had slipped through a back door with the help of airport staff and wanted to have a cup of tea and get his head down before flying north.

I opened the offices up at Edgeley Park at 7 am and soon got a call from Robbo saying he was boarding the shuttle. The airport was very busy at that time of the morning and I circled the block a few times before I saw the plane approaching. I parked up and was approached by a very tall angry looking traffic warden.

"Move that car now or I will book you," he bawled out.

I explained what I was there for and whom I was picking up.

"Well, in that case you have sixty seconds to get in the door and get him and his luggage in the car," he replied.

Out came Robbo, wearing his tracksuit but he had no luggage, the ground staff had not loaded it at the other end.

"Get in Robbo, before I get booked," I said.

Robbo sat in the passenger seat looked at me and said, "You should have seen the airport when we landed, anybody would think we had won the World Cup!"

I told him the Nation had been gripped by World Cup fever and that his life may change in that he was now a national hero.

"I could do with going to see Mally and Dimes [Jim Mallinder and Steve Diamond] and find out when I am back in training," he said.

Strange, I thought, and then he finished, "I would really like a Maddesons special too for my breakfast!"

Maddesons is a shop near Sale Sharks' old ground at Heywood Road and a special is a full English breakfast on a teacake, they are huge.

"See your dietary needs are the same pal?" I said.

"No change in that department Swanny, and can you buy them as I only have Australian currency with me?" he said.

I pulled into the car park at Heywood Road at around 8.30 am and Jason headed straight for Jim and Steve's office while I organised breakfast.

When breakfast arrived Robbo demolished his 'special' in double-quick time and thoughts of "it never touched the sides" came to mind.

I took Robbo to Edgeley Park and all the staff were delighted to see him and he was happy to see everyone again.

He sat in my office chair and I showed him the Press cuttings of the final and you don't need to be MENSA to work out which cutting he threw in the bin.

"Right Swanny, Amanda and the children are only back on Thursday so I am at a loose end tomorrow," he said.

"Well why not speak to the local press tomorrow and then you can relax before you go to pick up Amanda and the kids?" I said.

"Good idea, will you be here?" he said.

"No I am going to the States tomorrow for a five-day break but the staff here will look after you if I organise the press to come down." I replied.

"Fine, line them up but do me a favour and ask them to introduce themselves when they arrive and tell them not to let anyone in from *that* paper," he said.

"Still annoyed pal?" I asked.

"Not annoyed Swanny, just in a state of disbelief, I am not giving them any quotes to sell their papers after everything I have done for them." He replied.

"Okay Robbo, let me have a think about the paper while I am away, but I know I need to speak to Richard Prescott at the RFU later today," I said.

"I know I am piling jobs on you Swanny but can you drop my bags off at our house later on before you go home?"

The bags arrived in a taxi a couple of hours after Jason had left and they were very heavy. Fortunately I am used to heavy cases when I go away with Carole on holiday, as she packs everything when we travel.

I dropped the bags off at Robbo's house early in the evening and Robbo told me that when he arrived home there were several photographers waiting for him.

"Blimey, Robbo being stalked by the paparazzi what next?" I said.

Robbo smiled, shook my hand and said, "Have a great time Swanny, and I will text you to let you know how the presser goes on tomorrow."

When I arrived home my phone rang and a journalist asked me what time the Press Conference was being held the following day. I asked him which paper he wrote for, as it was not a name I knew, 'BINGO', he wrote for the paper that had caused Robbo grief the previous week.

Robbo is not a supporter of my Anglo-Saxon language skills but I lost it down the phone with the journalist who took it on the chin. He wasn't the journalist who had been 'door-stepping' the previous week, but I wanted him to report back on how we felt. The conversation was very one-sided and finished with the word 'off'!

The following morning when Carole and I were travelling to Manchester Airport I wondered whether the journalist I had ripped into would turn up. I need not have bothered wondering as I received a text message from Robbo telling us to "chill out and not to think about work!"

While in the departure lounge, Richard Prescott rang me. Rich had had a good night's sleep after his journey home on 'Sweet Chariot.'

"Swanny, I have just dictated a strongly worded letter to the Editor of Jason's favourite paper and asked them for an explanation and to tell them that the behaviour of their publication was not one that the RFU needed. Now Viva Las Vegas pal, go and enjoy yourself." The whirlwind trip of Las Vegas, Grand Canyon and Los Angeles was really tiring and when we arrived home five days later, I needed a holiday!

The weekend's game was against Cardiff Blues in the Heineken Cup and the Rugby World Cup victory had caught the imagination of the British public in that the Sharks' game was sold out three days in advance! 10,541 supporters would welcome Clive Woodward on to the pitch holding the trophy before the game and it was a day that I will remember for a long time.

Sky Sports had chosen the game for live transmission and the kick off time was 5.30 pm on a Saturday. Not a traditional rugby time, but everyone was still celebrating after the England victory.

Sale Sharks used to meet up at Heywood Road and travel by coach to Edgeley Park together. When the pre-match warm-up had ended the players returned to the dressing rooms for last minute instructions. Clive Woodward entered the arena holding the trophy and the whole stadium erupted, it was incredible. Flanked by three bouncers, Clive walked around the pitch and deservedly took the applause.

Robbo played on the wing and the first time he received the ball, you could feel the atmosphere lift to fever pitch. The supporters expected him to run the length of the field every time he touched the ball. The same can be said about Twickenham too. When a team has a hero the opposing fans usually "heckle and boo" them but Rugby Union, thankfully, is different, especially towards backs. Forwards like Martin Johnson and Lawrence Dallaglio get some stick but they are giants of the game and probably enjoy it!

Sale Sharks won a closely-contested game with a last-minute Charlie Hodgson drop goal. The place went crazy. Sale Sharks had a full house of 10,541, and there were loads of new fans in the ground. Robbo summed it up afterwards when he said, "People who are new to the game will think every game finishes with a drop goal, I'd better start practising!"

There was an incredible amount of PR for Jason to perform after the game and both my son Dan and I were shattered after everything was done, never mind Robbo who had run around for eighty minutes. He posed for photos with the World Cup, signed books, programmes, posters and shirts with a smile before we moved to the players' lounge for some food. Most of it had gone and so had his team-mates as, Robbo, Dan and myself sat down in a deserted lounge.

"Where is your car, Robbo?" I asked.

"Heywood Road," he replied.

Dan chipped in, "Robbo, I have just passed my test and I'm in my boy racer car, can I take you back to Heywood Road?"

Robbo smiled and said, "Go on then, it will be like old times! Should we wear baseball hats back to front?" Dan thinks the world of Jason and the feeling is mutual. The banter between them is hilarious at times and they keep in touch by phone regularly.

After the Cardiff win, the following week's Heineken Cup match was in Biarritz. The Sharks' problems started as soon as they got off the plane when a couple of players were injured in a practice session. Sharks lost heavily which meant they faced an uphill struggle to qualify for the Heineken Cup quarter-finals.

Robbo hardly had time to get his breath back after returning from France before he packed his bags to play in what many thought was a meaningless game at Twickenham a week before Christmas. The income from the game helped the RFU as they had not been able to host Autumn Internationals due to the World Cup, but to England the cost was high after Richard Hill was smashed in the face by an opponent in what was supposed to be an exhibition game. It was reported that Clive Woodward was not happy with the game being staged and I was just glad that Robbo escaped without being flattened.

The fixtures had given Sale Sharks a home game against Rotherham Titans the day after Boxing Day and even though Rotherham were cast adrift at the foot of the table almost 9,000 fans turned up for this festive clash. Rotherham took an early lead but Sharks hit back strongly and Robbo, playing in the centre, scored a try, his first of the season for the Sharks and his first since the World Cup Final.

After losing at Wasps early in January it was back to the Heineken Cup and mission impossible, playing away in Dublin against Leinster. The mood in the camp had been disrupted following a piece in the press about Jim Mallinder struggling to hold on to his position as Head Coach. It was well known that Jim's contract was due to expire at the end of the season, as was Steve Diamond's.

The players went to Leinster and it must be said played the game of their lives, winning 23-22 with a last-minute Charlie Hodgson drop goal. Brian Kennedy had flown to the game and dispelled rumours that Jim and Steve's jobs were under threat and even spent part of the game sitting on the bench with the two coaches.

After the game Brian boarded the team coach and thought it a good idea for the team to go and see the travelling supporters at their hotel. Robbo didn't fancy it, as he does not like going into bars and offered to look after Brian's young sons at the team hotel. Brian agreed and on the way back to the hotel, Jason ordered the coach to stop at a service station where he jumped out and came back with what was described as a "dustbin liner full of sweets" for his new role as child minder!

Robbo rang me from the hotel and asked me how the game had looked on television and how bad did Andy Titterrell's stamp on Eric Miller look. I told him that we had played well with plenty of belief and conviction and that the jury was out on Titts' stamp.

Andy was summoned to Dublin to answer a charge of stamping and was given a ban that would keep him out of the Six Nations despite the efforts of Club Chairman Quentin Smith who accompanied him to the hearing.

The following week Leinster made the return trip to play at Edgeley Park and again the ground was sold out. Stuart Pinkerton had retired after the game in Dublin and returned to Australia after two and a half years' great service with the club.

Sale Sharks played well but were dealt a blow when Charlie Hodgson hobbled off mid way through the first half. It was another setback in Charlie's career and this latest injury would keep him out for ten weeks. The Sharks lost the game 23-16 and worse was to come in the home game against

Biarritz the following week. Not only did the Sharks lose 15-0, not scoring for the first time in years, but scrum half Bryan Redpath received a bad shoulder injury and would miss the rest of the season. We also lost Mark Cueto with a thumb injury, which kept him out for a month.

The last group game was a formality away to Cardiff Blues as the Sharks were already out of the Heineken Cup. Robbo was benched for this game and the idea was only to use him in an emergency. The call to duty came on the hour and he raced on in the pouring rain and his first touch of the ball resulted in a knock on. The Welsh crowd gave him some stick but he reacted as he always did in a situation like this, he put in a couple of his special runs. Robbo will never say it but I believe he likes a bit of stick every now and again to give him extra motivation! I received a phone call early in the evening from Steve Diamond who said he had accepted an offer from Saracens to join their coaching staff.

Leicester Tigers were next up and it was going to be an interesting game as Sale Sharks had recorded a double at Welford Road earlier in the season. Leicester had their big guns in Johnson, Back, Kay, West and Corry back after the World Cup whereas Sale Sharks were without Mark Cueto, Charlie Hodgson and Bryan Redpath. Edgeley Park was full and the sleet and wind lashed the ground all day. I was amazed the game went ahead because the players could have drowned in some of the puddles on the pitch. Jason collected a high ball early in the game and was taken out in mid-air. I joked with him later that the way he came down in the water would have won him a silver medal in the Olympic diving event. The game finished in a 3-3 draw. After the game it was all hands to the pump as the players were in a bad way because of the cold and wet. We were distributing hot chocolate to players and wrapping them in blankets.

Robbo said, "Even in my days at Wigan playing at

Watersheddings, Oldham's old ground I have never been as cold and wet as I was tonight. When are we going to switch to summer rugby?"

I replied, "Talking of summer Robbo, I am off on holiday next week to Margarita and I am told it is thirty five degrees in the shade there."

The look on his face was a picture. "You just love to rub it in don't you pal? I am playing rugby while you are sunning yourself. I think I had better book myself on a sun bed while you are away," he said

"Robbo, people think I am your dad so I have to go and get my tan topped up every so often to be able to carry off the role," I said.

While I was away the local papers were 'mixing a bottle' with talk of Jim Mallinder's contract talks and unnamed players being unsettled. I spoke to Jason from my hotel in Margarita and asked what was going on. Jason told me that he had been away with England for most of the time I had been away but that the players needed to perform for Jim and show him the same respect as he had for them.

When I arrived back from Margarita I collected my bags from the carousel and turned on my mobile phone for the first time in a fortnight. Thirty-six text messages download-ed and then the phone rang. It was Niels de Vos asking me to drop Carole off at home and then drive to Edgeley Park.

I arrived, not having slept for thirty-six hours, smelling of suntan lotion and unshaven only to bump into Jason on the car park.

"Did it rain all the time you were there, pal?" he asked.

"No it was boiling hot," I replied.

"Couldn't resist that after you had rubbed my nose in it that you were going on a mid-winter holiday," he smiled.

The reason I had been ordered back to work was to rush out a press release that Jim Mallinder had signed a new deal with the club.

Saracens were the visitors on the following Friday in the Powergen Cup and the Sharks turned on the style winning 26-3. I couldn't resist saying hello to Steve Diamond who was sitting with his new boss Nigel Wray. In three years it was the first time Dimes had shaken my hand and called me David! As they say in cartoons, "exit stage right!"

Around this time the England World Cup squad were given MBEs for their World Cup victory and I listed Jason as Jason Robinson MBE in the programme, which got him some stick in the dressing room. The whole country was still in top gear after the win in Sydney and players were being offered the freedom of their home town almost every day. Stockport was different however, with people in the town saying he did not deserve any honour and was a well-paid sportsman. Robbo asked me to check into the freedom of the town for him and what it meant. I rang him and said, "Robbo, I have some bad news, not getting the freedom of Stockport means that you cannot walk with your sheep down the High Street!" I laughed.

"You're kidding me, is that what it means? I thought it meant I could get unlimited fast food or something useful, anyway I walk with my sheep in the local park!" he replied, by which time we were both in stitches laughing. People in the office in Stockport spent hours debating the issue of Jason when to be honest, he could not have cared less. Never mind, it filled some space in the local paper and kept some bigots happy for a short while.

Robbo was sharing his time between Cheshire and Middlesex as the Six Nations reached a climax. At the start of March I was told that Brian Kennedy had appointed Philippe Saint Andre as Director of Rugby and I picked Philippe up from the airport to take him back to the ground. Philippe asked if I had been on holiday and when I told him

I had been to Margarita, he said me that he had been there and his wife was born on the Caribbean island. Philippe told me he was a big fan of Jason Robinson and I said, "I know that, is that why the big animal of a forward you coached at Bourgoin targeted him?"

Phillipe laughed and said, "Ah, yes, Sebastien Chabal, he will be playing for Sale Sharks next season."

Philippe was great with all the media at the press conference. At Gloucester he had been criticised for speaking too much French, but he had worked on this and even showed he had developed an English sense of humour too!

I rang Robbo on the way home and told him that Philippe had been appointed as Director of Rugby. I also told him that Philippe was signing Chabal."

"Who's he?" Robbo asked.

"The big French bloke who played for Bourgoin who nearly cut you in half at Heywood Road," I said.

"Now that is a great signing, he can act as my minder!" Robbo laughed.

The next big game was the Powergen Cup semi-final in mid-March when Leeds Tykes were the visitors to Edgeley Park on a cold Saturday afternoon.

BBC Grandstand were broadcasting the game live from the 'beach' as Robbo referred to the Edgeley Park pitch. Robbo joked that to test the wind direction for kicking you usually throw a blade of grass into the wind but due to the lack of grass in Stockport he looked for flags flying to judge the best way to kick the ball.

Robbo was on fire in the game and scored a superb try as well as entertaining the crowd with some fantastic runs, which have become his trademark.

Tragedy struck just after half time when Sharks centre Graeme Bond was badly injured in a ruck. The game was halted for ten minutes while Graeme received treatment and was eventually carried off on a stretcher wearing a neck brace. It was in fact Graeme's last ever game for the club, as he had aggravated an old injury and although Graeme hoped he would play again, the specialists eventually advised against it.

Bondy and Jason were close in that Graeme said that one of the main reasons he had left Queensland in Australia was that he wanted to play alongside Jason. The sight of Graeme and Jason playing in the same side sent shockwaves throughout the Zurich Premiership in that they fed off one another going forward and were both very sound in defence.

Despite his injury Graeme stayed upbeat and the players kept in touch with him, but rugby players are a strange breed in that they don't get upset about a team-mate's injury, on the outside anyway. When a Sharks player is injured you never see the players milling round their crocked team-mate, they stay focussed for the restart.

After the semi-final Robbo rejoined his England team-mates down at Bagshot, but not before he won the team go-kart championships at the racetrack in nearby Didsbury. Robbo was undertaking opponents and was like a man possessed behind the steering wheel. The event was organised to get the players' minds off rugby for a few hours and was also excellent for team bonding. The 'awards' followed the event and Robbo paid tribute to Sir Clive Woodward for his victory. Why, he was asked? "All the driving around the M25 in getting to Bagshot honed my driving skills!" he replied.

The Powergen Cup final against Newcastle Falcons was a great day out and Robbo's sponsor, Mike Workman from Puma, had some special boots produced for him, with "Powergen Cup Final 2004" on the tongue of each boot.

Mike is a lovely man and a dedicated sponsor who is well respected by all the players at the club. He has some wonderful stories, which we have a laugh about whenever he visits the club. As a thank you for Mike I had a word with the BBC who had just started broadcasting their rugby magazine programme and put a pair of Robbo's boots up as a prize. Top people the BBC, they zoomed in on Robbo's boots after one of his legendary runs and Brian Moore made a comment about Robbo's new white boots. Job done, boots seen by millions and John Inverdale gave the boots away the following evening on the show.

The boots on the show were brand new in a box, but I had further plans and I gave Vicky Gommersall of BBC Look North West the pair Robbo had worn after the game for a competition.

The game was incredible from start to finish. Sadly Jonny Wilkinson was unable to play due to injury but there were seventy points scored in an end-to-end contest. Mark Cueto, Steve Hanley and Chris Mayor scored the Sharks tries and Charlie Hodgson kicked everything, but late in the game a Newcastle player, who sections of the press believed to be offside - now that is being tactful - charged down a Charlie Hodgson clearance kick and the Falcons scored the winning try.

After the game Jason was working with the younger players lifting them and the heartbreak of losing in a final got to some of the older ones too with Pete Anglesea in tears on the pitch.

Owner Brian Kennedy went round all the players and consoled them, before we asked them to do a walk around the pitch to thank the 15,000 fans that had made the journey from the North West.

The players did interviews for television and I caught a minute with Jason before he went to change.

Robbo was disappointed but said that we would be back and that we had done well in competition to beat Leicester, Saracens and Leeds en route.

Robbo decided to travel back with the team rather than with me in the car. I believe he knew he had a role to play with the squad and new Director of Rugby Philippe Saint Andre noted this.

The following Friday, Newcastle Falcons travelled to Edgeley Park to play in the re-arranged Zurich Premiership game and the Sharks smashed them 41-16 with Mark Cueto grabbing a hat trick.

After the game Robbo said to me, "Swanny remember 1998 when Wigan lost to Sheffield at Wembley, this tonight was so similar, we hammered them but we would swap to-night for last week if we could."

After the game Robbo asked me to drive him back to Heywood Road to pick up his car and driving down the M60 we both heard an incredible banging noise under the bonnet. "Strange, it's a new car and only done about 1000 miles!" I said.

When we parked up at Heywood Road we leapt out of the car and lifted the bonnet, Robbo making light of it said, "It's still got an engine so it should be okay, Swanny!"

We then looked at the wheels and to our amazement the wheels were loose, as the wheel nuts had not been tightened up at the pre-delivery inspection at the leasing company.

Typically Robbo said, "Imagine the papers Swanny, top media man defies death on motorway, giving a lift to his mate!" I laughed at the time but gave the leasing company both barrels the following day.

Sharks lost to Saracens the following week and needed to win at Leeds Tykes to secure a Wildcard place with a back-door chance of getting into the Heineken Cup.

Leeds were defeated 31-20 and Sale Sharks reward was a trip to Gloucester in the Wildcards. The Sharks were get-ting murdered at Kingsholm before Robbo took the game to them and scored an incredible hat-trick of tries to set up a grand finale. Sharks had clawed their way back playing 'crazy rugby', as Philippe calls it, throwing the ball about. Sadly Robert Todd of Gloucester got in on the act and intercepted a pass to sprint home. Toddy left Gloucester after the game to join Sale Sharks for the new season and has had some stick about that try, mainly from Jason and Mark Cueto who regularly remind Toddy that he is not as quick now!

Before the game I received a phone call from Malcolm Folley who had helped Jason write his autobiography. Malcolm was desperate to speak to Jason, so I asked why. He told me that he wanted to write a story that Jason would not be touring with England during the summer. Malcolm had become quite close to Jason and although Robbo is a private man, he has body language like anyone else and Malcolm said that he only wanted to speak to Jason for a minute for a quote. I told Malcolm it was not possible as Jason screens all his calls before a game and there was no way I was ringing him.

The following day the *Mail on Sunday* ran a 'flyer' that Robbo would pull out of the tour with fatigue. The piece quoted Amanda, Jason's wife and all the children's names as though it was a current, 'in touch' piece. Malcolm also wrote that he doubted Jason would tour with the Lions in 2005!

Sure enough, two days later, Sir Clive Woodward announced that Jason was taking the summer off, but not before I was battered with phone calls from the rugby writers, wanting to write the story before it was officially announced.

I had spent many hours helping Malcolm research Jason's autobiography and I am still at a loss to understand why he had to write the piece. I had in the past given Malcolm background information before he interviewed Jason, but that has never happened since.

On the Bank Holiday weekend Sale Sharks played the

Wildcard Final against Leicester Tigers at Twickenham, six weeks after the Powergen defeat. Leicester Tigers had been in turmoil all season, their coach Dean Richards had left and John Wells taken over. Leicester needed to win the game to gain a place in the Heineken Cup and were really up for the game. Sale Sharks, on the other hand, did well to name 22 players.

When the players arrived at the ground I was there to greet them and Robbo, captain for the day, looked at me. "Where do we change?" he said.

I knew then he was on his knees needing a rest; but he spoke to me as though I was a steward. I reminded him about it later but he could not remember the incident, gripped me round the shoulders and said, "Swanny I am shot, I have never been as tired in my life."

Sharks took an early lead with a Robbo try but Leicester Tigers cut us to pieces and ran out 48-27 winners. Sharks were hit with injuries too, Stuart Turner scratched his eye ball in a ruck and Andy Titterrell was in 'Disneyland' after his cheekbone collided with the back of Neil Back's head.

After the game I went to see how the injured boys were. Stuart Turner needed to go to hospital so two of our Community team, Ceri Wharmby and Darryl Griffiths took him. Andy Titterrell was all over the place with concussion. Dr Jones asked me to drive 'Titts' home but not to let him fall asleep. The Doctor told me that if he passed out that I was to turn off the Motorway and get him to a hospital asap!

Pete Anglesea joked, "Don't talk to him Swanny, you could send a glass eye to sleep!" I threw a bundle of socks at Pete and when he turned round he read my lips and could only make out the word "off".

Robbo said, "Swanny don't sing to him either, he is mixed up and I don't want him jumping out of the car at speed."

I helped Andy to the door and Robbo raced over. "Swanny

look after him, and give me a buzz tomorrow and let me know he is okay."

Andy is a great lad and I have known him since I joined the club. Hard as nails on the field but a gentleman off the pitch who will do anything to help the club.

When we got in the car Andy said, "Swanny when I get a knock to the head, I always sleep it off so wake me up in a couple of hours."

"But Titts, the Doc and Robbo said you have not to go to sleep!" I explained.

It went in one ear and out the other side and by the time we hit the M40, Andy was fast asleep.

He stayed that way until we reached Keele services when he sprung to life, took off his glasses, popped his contact lenses in and drank a bottle of Lucozade.

Just after the services the phone rang. It was Robbo. "Swanny, how's Andy? Put him on will you?"

Andy took the phone and said he was fine and that he was looking forward to having a sleep. He then passed the phone back to me.

Robbo thanked me and said that I could not lie to save my life and that he had worked out Titts had been asleep.

I checked in with Andy the following morning and he was a lot better and asked me to save the video of the game as he was catching a flight with England to the South Seas the following day.

Robbo called into the office a few days later and wanted to use the Internet.

"What are you buying now?" I asked.

"A house nearer the ground as I am weary of travelling to Cheshire every day for training," he said.

Robbo also told me that he was fed up with people ringing the bell on the gate asking for autographs.

"Public domain, Robbo," I said.

I can sympathise but told him to change his autograph from the usual work of art to an easier one then it would speed up the process.

"It's not their fault, it's just that after the last twelve months, I have had enough and have booked a holiday, for me Amanda and the children," he said.

"Get to Jamaica, they don't play rugby there and you can blend in!" I said.

"Swanny, never lose that ability to make me laugh pal, will you?" he said.

After he had left I was having a coffee with our Chief Executive Niels de Vos and was telling him that Robbo was a mess and needed a break.

Niels was sympathetic and in a way knew how he felt. He told me that when he was the Marketing Director at the Commonwealth Games in 2002, he would come home, sit in the chair and fall asleep sitting up.

I started preparations for the 2004-2005 season, planning the programme with my Press Officer John Everton, writing the club handbook and trying to find a day when we could have the Press day.

The mobile phone never displayed 'Billy Whizz' for about ten days until one morning it rang.

"Swanny, how are you pal? We are having a great time in Sardinia, and I am on the balcony looking at the sea, it's great," he said.

Thank goodness! I thought the batteries are recharged and he sounds like the Robbo I know!

"How have England been going on, how are season tickets going?" he asked.

"None of your business pal, you are on holiday, all I will say is that England have not had a good time," I replied.

"Just before I go Swanny, what day is it?" He asked.

"Thursday, why?" I asked.

"Great, I thought it was Tuesday, I have lost two days, I am coming home at the weekend so play some Lionel Richie on your show [referring to my BBC Radio Lancashire music show Sounds Like Saturday Night]," he said.

"No problem, dedicated to Amanda I suppose, are you still too tight to buy flowers then?" I said, happy he had returned to normal.

Philippe Saint Andre was a regular visitor to Edgeley Park for recruitment meetings with Niels and always popped into the office to find out what was going on. On one of his early visits he introduced me to his new coach Kingsley Jones, whom he had worked with at Gloucester and who was to join his other coach Jim Mallinder.

Philippe knew of my friendship with Jason and told me that he and Brian Kennedy had been discussing appointing Jason as Captain for the new season. Philippe wanted to know my thoughts on this and I said it would be a good move as Jason had played with some great players in both codes and under some great coaches and must have a wealth of knowledge.

We announced shortly afterwards that Robbo was the new captain and it was given a massive thumbs up by everyone apart from a few Sharks fans. Sale Sharks, like most clubs, have an unofficial fans' website and message board and one poster said that he thought it was a "marketing exercise by the club and was not a good appointment." Everyone is entitled to an opinion but one or two people weighed in with bitter comments. Message boards are a good idea in one sense but sadly it gives cowards a sounding board and I refer to it as the new century's answer to CB radio. Sale Sharks are very fortunate that we have a lot of great fans and have only a very small percentage of troublemakers, mainly on the message board. Robbo was delighted when he was told of his appointment and it added another dimension to his game.

"Swanny, I know I put on you a bit, but can you type up a

list of all the staff we have, what they do and their numbers, I want to have this on file and also displayed at the training ground," he said.

Robbo also contacted some of his Puma and Gillette contacts and organised some goods for the player of the month awards, a regular event at Wigan in his days at Central Park. He started to pay a lot of attention to everything that went on at the training ground and Philippe told me that he was really enjoying his extra responsibility.

"How many car parking spots do we get on game day, Swanny? Have we got a team room for pre-match? Can we get some heating in the dressing room?" he asked one day.

"Robbo, I never had as many problems when Bryan Redpath, Pete Anglesea and Alex Sanderson were captains!" I said.

"I want it to be right and I'll always be looking to improve," he winked.

Robbo wanted to finish his career at Sale Sharks and went to Brian Kennedy's home with Niels and Philippe to sort out the finer details. It only took a few minutes and with handshakes all round, Robbo told me that Brian invited Philippe and Niels to join him on the lawn with Robbo and Brian's lads for a game of touch rugby! That's the mark of Brian who is so passionate about Sale Sharks but likes to have a game of rugby too. Brian had a snooker room at his home and Jason signed him a limited edition print to put on display. Brian looked at the print and asked me to tell Jason to write something below the words "to Brian". It read, "Thanks for teaching me how to side step!"

Robbo obliged, laughing as he wrote the message but I know that Jason really respects Brian, because he was the man who took a huge gamble on him back in 2000, and it has paid off handsomely for all concerned.

CAPTAIN OF CLUB AND COUNTRY

The Press Day was the usual good fun and highly entertaining. The sun shone on Edgeley Park to which Robbo said, "Swanny the last time I was captain was with the Hunslet Under 11s and today is the first time I will be sitting at the front with the coaches. I have had a word with the big man upstairs and look at the weather, it's weather like I was used to in Yorkshire!"

"Robbo, I have been doing Press Days and photo calls for a few years now and it always sun shines for me, even when I organised one in Warrington in January!" I replied.

John Everton my Press Officer had organised how the team would line up on the official photographs, with the heights of players so that on the back row the tallest were in the middle and the line either side of the tallest (Dean Schofield).

Robbo took his position in the middle at the front between Philippe St Andre and Head Coach Kingsley Jones.

"Need a cushion to sit on Robbo, you look a bit small there in the middle," I said.

The squad thought it hilarious but Robbo hit back, "Swanny I am captain and I assumed I would have a ball to hold on this photo, you have let me down pal."

"It's here," I said, "Do you want a size four to make you look bigger?"

Getting a photo correctly taken with thirty-plus rugby personnel and staff on is a tall order but apart from the Adam Black and James Bramhall fiasco in 2001, all my Sale Sharks Press day photos have been fine. The other bonus with modern technology is the digital camera, so I could view the photo before getting the players in line for their head and shoulder shots.

Robbo had already commanded the respect of his troops and when he asked them all to face the camera and smile it was easy to stage manage. The army of photographers clicked away and the television crews, local and national, scanned the Sale Sharks' squad.

The head and shoulders shots were soon over and then several of the internationals were moved around the ground for sponsors' photographs. Jason is a natural at this in that he asks me beforehand who the people are, what they do and a bit of an insight into their company. He chats away and is respected for this.

The players were happily chatting to all the media when I noticed Jim Mallinder was quite distant from the proceedings. One of the journalists tipped me off that Jim was going to quit Sale Sharks as he had been offered a good job with the England Rugby Union Academy.

Sadly, Mally did walk away from Sale Sharks for good later that day to take up his new position. Jim was well liked by all the players and everyone at the club, from Brian Kennedy down. I spoke to Jason about it later and he just said to me that rugby is a short career and nothing stays the same for too long.

The players flew to France the following day for some hot weather training and practice games.

During the first game I was at home while Paul Smith, our Rugby manager, kept me updated. During the second half he told me that Robbo had taken a bad knock to his hip and was on his way to hospital. The French crowd had given him a standing ovation when he left the field as they respect a good player when they see one.

In situations like this everything goes through your mind: do I ring him; do I ring Amanda, his wife; how do we report

it? Dave Jones, the Club Doctor, rang me and said everything was in hand at their end and that Jason had spoken to
Amanda. Dave also told me that the x-rays had not found any
breaks but Robbo was in a lot of pain.

I put a note on the website that Sale Sharks had won the
game but Jason had gone off injured. The best thing to do
in situations like this is to be vague in reporting so as not
to alert future opponents. John Monie used this ploy in my
Wigan days. He said that being precise about an injury just
gave future opponents a free shot. Unfortunately you cannot
stop the over-inquisitive supporters! A Sharks supporter who
had travelled to France took it upon himself to contact the
media back home to say Jason had been badly injured. I was
furious, thinking that it could upset Jason's family and more
than anything it was not true.

I rang Robbo the following morning and asked him how
he was.

"Swanny, I am holding the hotel reception counter up at
the moment as I decided to do without my crutches but I am
really sore, and the worst bit about it is that Mark Cueto and
Steve Hanley are laughing at me and taking the mickey!"
he said.

Robbo took to the water for his rehabilitation even though
he hates swimming, but under the watchful eyes of Nick
Johnston, Head of Physical Preparation, and Phil Burt,
Physiotherapist, he recovered enough to act as a bottle carrier
for the final match of the French Tour. When the team arrived back the weather in the United Kingdom was glorious
and Robbo's hip injury improved daily. All the way through
his treatment he kept a keen eye on the players in his new
role as captain and regularly held meetings with Philippe and
Kingsley, preparing for the new season.

I have a strange collection of items in my office including
a talking model of Jim Royle of the Royle Family, Ozzy

Osborne and The Hood from Thunderbirds. One day before the season started Robbo looked at the model of The Hood, picked it up and said, "Swanny, can we take his hat off as it is a dead ringer for Nick Johnston? I want to take this to training to show Nick and as a marketing idea we could sell them in the club shop."

"Go on then, but bring it back," I said.

Within an hour the players arrived for a training session at Edgeley Park and they were falling about laughing at the Hood's striking resemblance to Nick Johnston. Nick is a good lad but he 'beasts' the players in training and had been nicknamed 'Zorba' as he looked a bit Greek. Nick, who is from Kendal, is responsible for getting the players in peak condition week in, week out.

The first game of the Zurich Premiership season paired Sale Sharks with Leicester Tigers at Edgeley Park. As usual, Leicester were tipped to finish top and Sale Sharks nearer the bottom than the top! The game was chosen as a televised game and shifted to Sunday afternoon at 1pm, as a curtain raiser to Johnny Wilkinson's comeback for Newcastle Falcons at Worcester. The problem with televised games at Edgeley Park is that the trucks take up half the car park and the players have to park away from the ground. Robbo gave me some grief down the phone and face-to-face saying that the players should be able to park at the ground. I held firm on the car parking arrangements though and promised to review it for the next televised game. I wouldn't say we fell out about the car parking arrangements but it was easy to see that Jason was taking his captain's responsibilities very seriously.

Robbo said, "I have played under some great captains, including Shaun Edwards, Andy Farrell, Dean Bell, Bryan Redpath, Pete Anglesea and Martin Johnson and I have picked up some ideas over the years, so hopefully I can put their leadership skills to good use."

The players arrived early as arranged and had their pre-match meeting in one of the suites adjacent to the main stand. The tunnel walls displayed action photographs of the Sale Sharks players at the request of Philippe and Kingsley and the dressing rooms had been cleaned thoroughly during the close season as part of the ground facelift I had organised. We also had some heating installed in the home dressing room to make the players feel comfortable when they arrived for games during the winter.

The stage was set for the season opener but less than 7,000 turned up for the game, probably because of the strange kick-off time. Leicester Tigers didn't bring too many fans but with the railway station at Stockport closed for maintenance work, supporters had to rely on cars and coaches.

When kick-off time arrived the temperature was around ninety degrees and it soon became apparent that Sale Sharks' pre-season preparations organised by Nick Johnston had worked. Sebastien Chabal was incredible at the back of the pack on his league debut and the backs responded superbly. Bryan Redpath, Mark Cueto and Jason all scored tries and Sale Sharks ran out 26-19 winners.

The following week Sale Sharks travelled to Wasps, the current Champions, and a section of the game's media men were not so keen on writing off the Sharks after the win over Leicester.

The Sharks won 33-30 thanks to a late Charlie Hodgson goal but Sale had opened their scoring with a Jason Robinson drop goal after four minutes. It was his first since dropping a goal on the stroke of half time for Wigan against St Helens in the first season of Summer Rugby League.

After the game I spoke to Robbo as I always do and went through it with him. He told me, "Toddy owed us that try after that one at Gloucester last season. Stan [Steve Hanley] is a great finisher and Charlie is back to his very best."

Next up were Saracens who didn't offer a lot and Sale Sharks were top of the Premiership with three out of three. Back-to-back home games saw Worcester Warriors demolished 57-3. The Sharks scored eight tries and again Robbo was on the scoresheet with a try. The coaching that the players were receiving from Philippe, Kingsley and Mark Nelson was paying off and the supporters began to believe that something could be on this season.

Mark Cueto was called up for England training around this time and we were all naturally delighted that he had, at last, been recognised and had a chance of playing for England in the Autumn Internationals. Jason was particularly pleased for Mark whom he had spent many hours helping with his game. Mark is a great player and is willing to do anything to promote the club by attending supporters' evenings or coaching sessions for children and he has one of the best attitudes I have ever experienced in my ten years in sport.

While the Internationals are away, early in the week, training is very fragmented as rugby sessions are almost pointless. One Wednesday early in October I took our work placement student Hahmed Esfahanian down to the training ground for the weekly media day. While talking to Philippe there was an incredible commotion and when I looked round Hahmed was entertaining the squad by dancing! "Great," I said, "just what I need this, the media are all here and there's Hahmed, who wants to be a journalist, bopping around break dancing!"

I was about to wade in and stop Hahmed when I realised the players were having a great time and Steve Hanley had tears in his eyes with laughter. Apparently, Hahmed had been sitting with reserve hooker Johnny Roddam and had been watching MTV. Hahmed had told Johnny he could dance better than the performers on the televison and Johnny had goaded him into 'entertaining the troops'.

Philippe said Hahmed was crazy but he was glad his players liked it because it had made them happy. Philippe said Hahmed had to leave though, because he had to prepare his players for the weekend's game.

While driving home my mobile phone rang, it was Robbo.

"Swanny, news has filtered down here to the England training camp that you organised cabaret at lunchtime. Steve Hanley rang and texted us to say it is a 'must see' and you as his agent can organise it for a repeat performance next week!" Robbo said laughing.

We had a tough-looking game at Headingley the following weekend and Leeds Tykes would not lie down and die. Sale Sharks were fortunate to win 14-11 to keep the unbeaten run going. After the game Robbo was hijacked on the pitch by autograph hunters and after spotting this I made sure Carole was in a lounge before wading in to rescue Robbo. Ed Marriage of BBC Five Live wanted an interview with Jason so I made the excuse to the people wanting Jason's signature that the BBC had a deadline and that he would sign the rest of the autographs later. It's a situation I don't like as I always collected autographs as a kid and know how much it means, but after running about for eighty minutes Jason deserves a break and a sit down. Robbo did the interview for Ed and we both thanked him for requesting the interview as it had got him off the pitch.

After showering and changing Jason signed the remaining autographs as he had promised. View From, the clothing range that Marks and Spencer owned, had paid for some player cards and I had about two hundred in my pocket, pre-signed, but autograph hunters usually want a specific item signed. Jason's mail arrives at Edgeley Park daily and it is all answered with photos or letters but he now refuses to sign photographic prints unless they are personalised due to

Internet auction sites offering signed Robbo items for hundreds of pounds. It is an issue he is not happy with and I must say I cannot really blame him.

Dance day arrived and I had an early morning call from Jason who had organised the whole event and had even brought with him an old shellsuit retrieved from his attic for Hahmed to wear. The players finished training and were almost fighting to use the showers to get washed and changed for the cabaret.

Jason had organised the day around the Player of the Month awards and took to the floor after lunch to tell the players what was in store.

Hahmed had gone along with it all and had changed into Robbo's old sky blue shellsuit and entertained the boys for about ten minutes before getting a standing ovation from everyone. The press, who were also present, must have been impressed by the togetherness of the whole squad and that Philippe allowed it to happen, although he just shook his head in disbelief.

Hahmed became an instant hero and when I told the players he wanted to interview some of them to build up his media portfolio they were delighted to help. Hahmed left the club having interviewed Jason, Mark Cueto, Steve Hanley, Charlie Hodgson, Chris Jones and Andy Titterrell as well as becoming a friend on first-name terms with Jason.

After a blip, narrowly losing at home to London Irish, Sale Sharks ran riot at Northampton and won 23-6 with Mark Cueto and Andrew Sheridan scoring tries. Robbo told me it was a brutal match with blood flowing regularly and the game finished with uncontested scrums. Sale Sharks had always had a reputation of having fantastic backs but lacking strength in the forwards but the new regime of Philippe and Kingsley were making the rugby media and supporters up and down the country take notice.

Robbo had a break over the next fortnight because the International players were rested in the opening round of the European Challenge Cup against Catania. The thoughts of Sicily in October excited the players but I had heard that the island was full of 'strange goings on'. I was just happy the players all arrived back safely and in the second leg the job was finished with a 50-3 victory. Unfortunately this game turned out to be Trevor Woodman's last for Sale Sharks as he received a bad dead leg to add to his ongoing back problem. Trevor hobbled off at the interval and ten minutes into the second half I noticed he had not returned to sit on the bench. I made my way to the dressing room and he was standing looking at his trainers. I realised he could not bend down to put them on because he was in so much pain, so I helped him put his trainers on and he took a seat in the stand.

I liked Trevor and he was so unlucky with injuries so soon after arriving at the club. We regularly had a chat over coffee and he would tell me some great stories about Robbo, who he and Phil Vickery had nicknamed 'Stumpy'. I remembered that one and asked Robbo a few weeks later why 'Stumpy'. He just laughed and said, "You've been talking to Trevor again, haven't you?"

Trevor was a regular spectator at Edgeley Park and on the surface his spirits were high, but he was a World Champion unable to play with his new team-mates. It must have been hard to take in and accept. Jason kept in touch with Trevor as did several of the players and I rang him to check he was all right.

Robbo returned for the Newcastle Falcons game on Bonfire Night as the first full house of the season packed into Edgeley Park. Before the game rumours were rife that Jason would be offered the England Captaincy in the absence of the injured Johnny Wilkinson. I won't say when I got to hear the news had been confirmed but I rang Jason to ask him if he needed business cards with "Jason Robinson MBE, Captain of England" on! He just said, "Not bad for a lad from Hunslet and do you know, Swanny, I don't even know all the rules yet!"

"Are you going to be like Martin Johnson and give the players a rousing speech before they take the field?" I asked.

"Martin is a one-off and has the height and looks to carry it off and make you listen. He is an incredible bloke and a great Captain, I am only filling in until Johnny comes back," Robbo replied.

The following week Sale Sharks played at Bath, without all the Internationals and lost 27-13. After the match Sebastien Chabal found himself cited by the Match Commissioner for illegal use of the feet in the ruck. I have been involved in Rugby Union for five seasons and must say that I thought it was harsh. Chabal got a two-match ban for his sins, much to the disgust of the Sale Sharks fans who made him a folk hero from day one.

England hammered Canada in the first of the Autumn Internationals with Mark Cueto and Andrew Sheridan making impressive debuts, and Robbo led his troops superbly. A great story came from the reception after the game. An old General type had been talking rather loudly to his friend and said, "That Jason Robinson is a good player but until today I hadn't realised he was black!"

The following week was a bad time for both Robbo and myself. My wife Carole was admitted to hospital with stomach pains and was kept in for some tests. Robbo was on the phone regularly asking how she was and helped me a lot, as I was upset seeing Carole in such pain. She was released after a couple of days and Jason was first on the phone to have a chat with her to ask her how she was.

The next day, Robbo rang. He was not a happy man. The media 'dirty tricks' squad who had not surfaced since the

World Cup Final had moved away from their troughs and were at it again. They were visiting Jason's family and one clown even tried to get an interview saying that Jason had said it was okay for them to talk to him! Sian and Clifford at Octagon were doing their best with their media contacts and then came the bombshell, Jason had decided that he would not do any media work on the build up to the game. Andy Robinson, the new England Head Coach, was very supportive, Dee McIntosh and Richard Prescott of the RFU Communications Department were very professional and like me tried to talk Robbo out of his decision but ultimately accepted and respected it.

I tried to talk him round but he said, "Swanny, I bend over backwards to help these people with interviews and photographs and don't see why I should help them if this is the way they treat me."

"But Robbo," I replied, "you have a good working relationship with the media guys and they are disgusted by the way their own papers have treated you."

"I am not budging on this," Robbo said, "the people who have done this are a disgrace and I don't see why I should do interviews for them to sell papers for people to buy and the money that pays their wages. I am making a stand and that is it."

Sky Sports was Jason's first interview of the week, which was done on the pitch an hour before the kick off. He was focussed and was not comfortable with the interview. I sent a text to Robbo at this stage and asked him to ring me before he did the Press Conference after the game. He did and I said I had worked out what the press were going to ask about first and it wasn't the result!

"Swanny I am only going to talk about today's game and next week's game against Australia, if they want to know all about me and my past they can buy the book *Finding My*

Feet," was Robbo's reply.

I was Christmas shopping with Carole when my mobile went off. It was Chris Foy of the *Daily Mail*, who usually acted as shadow writer for Jason's column in the paper. Chris is a very good journalist who had written Jason's column well in the past and he told me that Jason would not answer his calls.

"Can you blame him? He is not talking to *any* of the media this week," I said.

After the game Jason attended the Press Conference with Andy Robinson and would only talk about the game as he had said he would. Dee McIntosh the England Media Manager and Richard Prescott, Director of Communications with the RFU, helped Jason all they could, but on this occasion he didn't need help."

The following week England lost to Australia in a closely-fought game and the knives were out, not only for Jason but Charlie Hodgson, whom a section of the press thought had cost England the game with his goal kicking. Jason is very close to Charlie and helped him through, although Charlie is a proud lad from Halifax who took the criticism in his stride.

When the players returned north after the Australia defeat, I met up with Jason at the training ground in Bramhall. He told me that he would honour his contract with the *Daily Mail* but he would not be renewing the deal as he didn't feel comfortable writing a column for any national paper.

On the Wednesday morning I was in my office early and Robbo rang me. "Swanny, I have got to tell you this it's so funny. I went to my old house yesterday to let someone in and when I set off back to Cheshire I realised I didn't have enough money to get some fuel, I'd left my wallet at home. I legged it to the petrol station and the can was going to cost me more than I had with me so I went to the hardware shop on Leyland Lane, he loaned me some money and took me back to my car in his van," he said laughing.

"Wish I had had a camera... Captain of England and Sale Sharks, World Cup winner and MBE, brilliant," I replied. I was also delighted he had let the problems of the previous week with the Press flow straight over his head.

The Sale players travelled to France the following Thursday to play Narbonne in the second round, first leg of the European Challenge Cup. Director of Rugby Philippe Saint Andre was taking nothing for granted in this competition and wanted to win the trophy. Sale Sharks won 33-15 with Jason dropping a goal and Steve Hanley scoring a try, which meant that Mark Cueto had to act as personal servant to Jason and Steve the following week. Jason forgets nothing and put Mark through his paces, ordering small quantities of food, often just to get his own back. He had set up an arrangement with Steve and Mark at the start of the season which said that whichever of them didn't score had to wait on the other two for a week. Mark was scoring tries for fun, as was Steve so the first opportunity that Robbo got to get his own back on Mark, he milked it. The arrangement only worked when one out of three didn't score and it was great to witness any one of the most prolific back lines in the game with a napkin over their arm waiting on. The win in Narbonne was not without its problems - Bryan Redpath broke his cheekbone when he banged heads with Andrew Sheridan. Robbo believed it was the worst possible scenario banging into Sherry who just rubbed his head while Bryan was in pieces!

Sale Sharks finished off Narbonne the following week at Edgeley Park and then Plymouth Albion were next up as visitors in the Powergen Cup. Robbo was rested, as Philippe knew the team had some tough games ahead. Robbo did his bit pre-match and sat in the stands with the coaching staff.

He watched every ruck, maul, tackle and kick and was so focussed during the game that he didn't notice people asking for his autograph.

The Christmas game against Bath was sold out before the staff broke up for the festive break and Philippe billed the game as a 'must win well game'. Sale Sharks scored three first-half tries and went in with 19 points on the board but failed to break down Bath in the second period to finish 19-10 winners. The match was spiteful with a lot happening off the ball and was a dress rehearsal for the Powergen Cup quarter-final game four weeks later.

The first game of 2005 was away to Newcastle Falcons who had Jonny Wilkinson fit again. I mentioned to Jason that Saracens and here were the only grounds on which we had never won in the professional era.

"Thanks for that Swanny, that's a big incentive for us. Let's see if we can end the run."

The score changed hands regularly and Newcastle scored early with a Matthew Tait try after Jason lost his footing when attempting to tackle the big Falcons centre. So annoyed was Jason that he scored an incredible solo effort try on the half hour. He picked up the ball ten metres in his own half and sidestepped, dummied, sprinted and swerved his way to a try under the posts. Not satisfied with that, he scored another soon after. Sale Sharks led 29-23 going into stoppage time when Jonny Wilkinson burst through the last line of defence to score under the sticks and then convert. Sale Sharks were beaten 30-29 and the following day most of the papers ignored Jason's try but concentrated on putting Jonny on a pedestal. Some didn't mention the team they were playing and that Charlie Hodgson, who kicked seven out of seven, had outplayed Jonny for most of the game.

You have to feel sorry for Jonny, though, because he is a great player and attracts media coverage like a magnet.

However, I sometimes feel that sections of the media are just waiting for him to miss a crucial kick and they will crucify him. Jason has the utmost respect for Jonny and quite rightly so - a fit Jonny Wilkinson is a World-class player.

Sale Sharks regrouped and faced Agen at home in the European Challenge Cup quarter-finals five days later. Agen took an early lead and for a while Sale Sharks' run in the competition looked to be coming to an end. During the first half Sebastien Chabal put in one of the biggest hits I have ever seen on the Agen fly half. The Agen players overre-acted and there were twenty-four players going at it hammer and tongs in the middle of the pitch. The referee sinbinned Chabal, which was an incredible decision because the video showed he had taken him out legally. We won the game 34-18 and looked forward to finishing the job off in France. Jason took an age to change and had to sign some items in my office before he joined his team-mates for his meal. He was laughing all the way to my office, which meant he was up to something but told me he would tell me what was amusing him when we got there. He signed the shirts and photos and I said, "Go on Robbo, what's so funny?"

He stood in front of me, took hold of the bottom of his suit trousers, to reveal that he had odd shoes on!

"How bad's that Swanny, I packed my bag last night and it was dark. The good thing is that they are a similar design but one has laces and the other doesn't!"

I suggested he wear his trousers like hipsters and he would be okay. I also told him that when I wrote my book it would get a mention!

On my way home to Chorley, the phone rang: it was Robbo.

"Swanny, I have never been so nervous in my life, I hoped nobody knew that I had odd shoes on but thankfully I car-ried it off," he said.

He continued, "What about that tackle Sea Bass [Chabal] made? Tell you one thing, I am glad he is on my side. You know, as a back, when you look at some of the forwards you have to run through and the treatment you get, it gives me a buzz watching our forwards perform. We have a good set of players Swanny, this could be our year!"

We have conversations like this after most games as we are both driving home. I am wound up having had a fifteen-hour day and it's good to talk rugby. I prefer away games as I am able to watch the whole game and my only jobs are to look after the coaches and players with the press.

The following Monday I received a text message from Jason saying he was in bed ill with flu and felt awful. As the week wore on he got no better and the team departed without him. The idea was that Jason would fly out in Brian Kennedy's private jet on the day of the game but Jason was too ill to travel. He had to rely on text messages to keep him updated. Sale Sharks lost the game 17-15 but won on aggregate to set up a semi-final against Connacht.

Up to the following Friday the treble of Zurich Premiership, European Challenge Cup and Powergen Cup was still on. Bath were our next opponents, in the Powergen Cup quarter-final. Jason had not fully recovered from the flu but pronounced himself fit. Philippe had spoken to him and asked him to play as long as he could before being replaced. Charlie Hodgson hobbled off in the first half but Robbo was showing no signs of fatigue after climbing out of his sick bed. On the hour Robbo made a burst from the halfway line and was eventually hauled down fifteen metres short of the Bath line. When he got up he was hobbling badly and had to be replaced. Sharks led comfortably at this stage but Bath finished strongly and won with the last kick of the game.

Jason was in the dressing room peeling off his wristbands and I sat with him. He told me he had caught a stray knee on his hamstring and it was aching. Dr Jones and the backroom team moved in and applied ice and then assessed the injury. The Doctor told me he would be fine, as it was bruising, not a tear.

I helped Jason to his car via the back way and he drove home, shattered. He should, with hindsight, have cried off but he respected the coaching team of Philippe, Kingsley and Mark Nelson as well as his team-mates and wanted to play.

The following morning I woke up and showered before having my breakfast. I was due at Edgeley Park for a Stockport County game to work as Media Manager. Carole made breakfast and I turned on the television in the kitchen. I nearly choked on my toast when the news said that Jason had been badly injured in the defeat to Bath and was very doubtful for the opening game in the Six Nations against Wales at the Millennium Stadium.

My first reaction was to turn up the television then flick onto the text section where sure enough Robbo was lead story.

I thought I was losing my touch and the press had got a story without me knowing. With a mouthful of toast I rang Robbo expecting it to be on answer phone. I would leave him a message and then find out how we are going to deal with this news.

To my surprise he answered, "Morning Swanny, just listening to the Drifters CD you got for me," he said.

"How are you pal?" I asked

"Leg's a bit sore, going in for some physio and a soak in the spa. The good thing is I slept well but I will be ready for Northampton next week," he said.

"Hang on, have I missed something here? The television is saying you have such a bad injury you might miss the Wales game," I said.

"News to me Swanny, tell you what, put out a quote

from me saying I got a bang on my hamstring but am looking forward to leading the boys out next Saturday against Northampton," he said

I drove to work smiling, mixing a bottle for the source of the doom and gloom news and by the time I parked up at Edgeley Park, I had the whole Press release in my head.

After firing up the laptop in my office I couldn't type it quick enough and had to use spellcheck, as my left hand was not working in tandem with my right.

Suffice to say the whole story disappeared faster than the Titanic. The fact I had quoted Jason personally made the media listen, and by jumping the gun the television station that ruined my breakfast had been paid back with interest. Bizarrely, the reporter who filed the copy rang me and asked if he could interview Jason now that he had recovered!

Robbo was buzzing during the week in preparation for the game against Northampton. He was back to his normal best, joking and winding up anyone he could. One incident involved Lisa Robinson, who runs the club merchandise store. Lisa is a good friend and is the longest-serving member of staff at the club. Jason always jokes that he can avoid anyone with his side step, except Lisa who can always stop him when she wants merchandise signing. Jason respects the phenomenal amount of work Lisa does and jokes that they are brother and sister but with different dads!

Lisa rushed into my office red faced and couldn't get her words out for laughing. Eventually she said, "I am going to kill Robbo when I see him!"

"Why, what's he been up to?" I replied.

"I got this call and the voice said that they wanted to buy some action photos of Mark Cueto. I told them I didn't have any and that they should ring you. The bloke said he wasn't ringing you, as you are rude and unhelpful. I suggested he ring Clint Hughes, but he said his pictures were blurred and it went on for about five minutes, before he cracked and started laughing… it was Robbo," she said.

"Back to his best then, we had better watch out," I said.

Peter Jackson, Ian Stafford, Steve Bale and Alastair Hignell all phoned to book press passes for the game, which was being played on the Saturday afternoon as a live Sky TV game. They all wanted a word with Robbo in readiness for the England game in Wales.

"No problem Swanny, we will do it in the tunnel after I change, let's do them all at once."

True to his word he appeared half an hour after the game finished and the press got their stories. The good thing about the Rugby Union Press is that they are mostly full-time writers and broadcasters and are easy to work with. They respect privacy and rarely ring me "after the office closes".

I stood nearby clutching a bundle of signed autographed cards for Robbo to distribute and wrote on a piece of A4, "Tell them I am holiday next week Robbo," and held it up so Robbo could read it.

"Swanny is going on holiday next week to the Caribbean, St Lucia in fact, and would like you to know that you can ring him anytime, day or night! When I pack up playing I'm going to be a Media Manager and you can quote me on that," he laughed.

After the media had left and the autographed cards given out Robbo and I sat on the front row of the main stand and 'chewed the fat' for five minutes.

He told me to have a good break and said he would be in touch.

"Remember Robbo, I will be four hours behind UK time," I said.

"I remember you forgetting the time difference when I was in New Zealand, Swanny, I'll be in touch," he laughed.

On the Monday morning I received a text message that

said, "Enjoy your break Swanny from Robbo and the England Boys." I rang him while we waited in the departure lounge and he asked me to bring back some Jerk Sauce for his barbecue and a Rasta hat (one in Jamaican colours with dreadlocks stitched around the edge).

St Lucia is a beautiful island and the hotel was perfect. The only downside was that the English newspapers cost $7 a day and were on A3 photocopied sheets! No copyright problems here, I thought!

As the weekend neared the pressure was on the England boys to deliver. Sadly England lost to Wales who eventually went on to win the title. Robbo drove to Reading the following day to watch the lads carve out a great revenge victory against London Irish. The following Saturday England lost to France and the heat from the media was warmer than the Caribbean sun!

After the French defeat I was getting ready to go for dinner in the hotel when the mobile rang. It was Robbo. He told me the team had been unfortunate to lose to France and although the team had lost both games, they had not been hammered. I sat on the balcony and we talked through the players who were missing or who had retired from the World Cup-winning side. We agreed that the team was in transformation. We talked for about ten minutes and before we said goodbye Robbo told me that Sebastien Bruno had given Mark Cueto a clip around the ear and Mark wanted to have a go back! We laughed and said it was not advisable but then again Mark is a fierce competitor and never takes a backward step! I put the phone down and before we left the room I'd got a text message saying, "Don't forget my Jerk Sauce and my hat, Swanny!"

When I arrived home I downloaded my emails, all 2,448 of them, and checked the club website to catch up with everything. I had been been moody all day, mainly through tiredness but also because the papers I had read on the plane had headlines saying that Charlie Hodgson was a choker and couldn't play in big games. I rang Robbo to ask him how Charlie was and he said he was fine and suggested I ring Charlie to catch up with him.

Charlie is another player who has had his critics and was not happy with comments made on television. I suggested to Charlie that he should take a media break that week and that I would be back at work the following day to look after him. One of Charlie's biggest critics at the time was Sky Sports pundit Stuart Barnes. Barnsey plays Devil's advocate and has a job to do just like Mike Stephenson with Rugby League. Stuart was a great player with Bath and Bristol, though he did not get the number of caps he deserved, but he is prone to stirring the pot to create reaction. But in Stuart's defence he also rates Charlie highly and gives credit where credit is due. The person I feel sorry for most is Miles Harrison. Miles is a first-class commentator but he has to share a commentary box with Barnsey every week.

At the training ground Mark Cueto told me about the clip that Sebastien Bruno had given him and that they had eyeballed each other when they had arrived for Sale Sharks training the day before.

Leeds Tykes are an ever-improving side and while Sale Sharks beat them 19-10 they knew they had been in a tough game.

The international players left after the Leeds victory and without them, successive defeats at Worcester and Saracens threatened to wreck the Sharks' plans.

There was worse to come. Robbo injured his hand in losing to Ireland at Lansdowne Road. He had played for 75 minutes with the injury but after the game the doctors wanted him to go for a scan. The scan revealed a bad ligament injury and an operation was necessary. I worked closely with Dee McIntosh and Richard Prescott at the RFU, as we wanted the club and England press releases to be issued at the same time. Getting this right can be hard work but this time it worked well with a 3-2-1 down the phone and a left click on the computer mouse!

Robbo had the operation at Wrightington Hospital on the outskirts of Wigan and he needed general anaesthetic for the operation. He was fitted with a pot on his right arm and the only positive for a few weeks was that he couldn't sign any autographs! Not that he ever refuses a signature but I am sure it was a relief.

Good Friday saw London Wasps visit Edgeley Park and they were on fire during the first half, building up a massive lead. Jason was bottle carrying on the Vernon Side of the ground, opposite the main stand and was bawling instructions to his team-mates. Sale Sharks, aided by a half-time roasting from Philippe and Kingsley, clawed their way back into the game and only failed to tie the scores when Mike Hercus saw his last-minute kick deflected wide by a Wasps player's arm.

After the game I had set up a PR exercise weeks before and was very grateful that Robbo could help out. I had worked as MC at the Leyland and Farington Cricket Club pre-season dinner and I auctioned a prize where the lucky bidder would meet Jason after a game, get a signed print and his kit. Jason was a star and Stephen Ward and his family from Leyland had a great evening as his guests. The cricket club is very special to me as it was where I was introduced to the game as a seven-year-old. The prize had helped the cricket club raise necessary funds for their forthcoming season. The following week Robbo asked me to write a letter to the club wishing them all the best for 2005. He signed it and it was photocopied and displayed around the ground at Fox Lane.

The following day Robbo rang me at home and told me

the Doctor had passed him fit and he would return to action the following week in the European Challenge Cup semi-final in Galway against Connacht. This news was kept from the media until the Wednesday before the game but once the media had received the press release from Edgeley Park; it was wall-to-wall Robbo, just as I like it. Although the European Challenge Cup is a secondary competition to the Heineken Cup, Jason Robinson is news and the game in Connacht was taking pride of place in the press.

The game in Galway was tough and Jason was the first to admit he was a little rusty, but showed signs that he was fresh after his enforced break. Sharks won 25-18 with a powerful performance up front while try-scoring machine Mark Cueto bagged a brace.

The Sharks were hammered at Leicester Tigers the following week 45-15. Steve Hanley and Mark Cueto told me Robbo had lost it in the dressing room at the break after Sharks had conceded four tries in fifteen minutes. I must admit I would like to have seen Robbo with all guns blazing! Sharks were more committed after the turnaround, with Robbo's roasting ringing in their ears.

The defeat with no bonus points left Sale Sharks with an uphill struggle to stay in the top four and to achieve one of the goals of reclaiming a Heineken Cup place.

The press day at Stockport Rugby Club the following Wednesday was a very low-key affair. It was a case of getting the press in and out as soon as possible. Philippe, Kingsley, Mark and Jason wanted full focus on the game against Gloucester which was a five point must win - four for the win plus the bonus point - occasion.

Gloucester didn't stand a chance. 9,500 Sale Sharks fans roared on their heroes and Sebastien Chabal was incredible, bossing the game from the start. He was making yards every time he picked up the ball and picking up players who were as heavy as he is and dumping them on the soggy pitch. Jason bossed the backs and the smile on the Sale Sharks players' faces after the game was a joy to see. Robbo gave one of his rousing speeches after Philippe and Kingsley had finished their debrief and Brian Kennedy congratulated the players for putting the Sale Sharks locomotive back on track.

Connacht were the next visitors to Edgeley Park the following Sunday and the media believed they had a chance. Sale Sharks systematically smashed Connacht to run up 59 points their biggest win of the season. The win earned Sale Sharks a Cup Final place against Pau, but that was on the back burner.

Sharks' Marketing Manager Nathan Bombrys organised a Tetley's fans' night at Edgeley Park and part of the evening was a forum with Bryan Redpath, Mark Cueto, Jason White and Jason Robinson on the panel. I was asked to chair it. I had been winding up the lads on the panel and they in return were giving me some stick with text messages.

There were four hundred people present and I introduced the panel, first Bryan then Mark then Jason White and then Robbo. The questions from the audience were excellent, but there were a lot of duplication so I started having some fun, first with Bryan then referring to Mark as Frank - which is his unwanted nickname - then it was my chance.

"Tell me Jason, do you think there should be any rule changes next season?" When Robbo picked up the microphone and started to answer, I cut in. "Excuse me, I was talking to Jason White," I said with a wink.

Robbo responded superbly. "Are you looking for a fight?" he asked.

The audience loved it and I countered by saying, "Go on then, and you can throw the first punch!"

The whole evening was a great success, Nathan gave a presentation to all the amateur clubs present and his community team worked the floor to look after the assembled Rugby supporters.

When the evening had wound up Jason came into my office to sign off some of his mail and we had a great laugh about the forum. Jason refuses engagements to speak publicly and we have in the past done a double act where I feed him the questions and he answers. I have told him we should take the show on the road, who knows, maybe one day?

The last week of the regular Zurich Premiership season was full of twists and turns and 'what happens ifs'. Quite simply, if Sale Sharks won at Harlequins they would be in the Heineken Cup in 2005-2006. Saracens were the form team and I am sure the players were aware that Saracens could have overtaken them and that Steve Diamond would have given them grief for a long time to come!

Harlequins started well, playing for their Premiership lives and scored three first-half tries. Charlie was kicking his points and Steve Hanley scored a great try at the end of the first half. Quins tired late on and Mark Cueto scored an incredible try to win the game for Sale Sharks. Looking at the try on the video there is a similarity with Jason's running technique and it was pleasing to see all the Robbo influences were rubbing off on Mark. Mark was happy on camera but deep down he was hurting like hell. He had been down for a couple of weeks because he had not been called up for the British Lions tour to New Zealand, a decision which shocked everyone in the game except Sir Clive Woodward who picked the squad. Robbo had helped Mark cope with his heartbreak and I spent time with Mark telling him to let his rugby do the talking and if he carried on scoring he could not be overlooked, especially now that Iain Balshaw was struggling after the injury he suffered playing for Leeds Tykes. I must admit I had my doubts though, as Mark should have been in the original squad and wondered whether Sir

Clive Woodward had a downer on him; after all, he never used him after the tour of Argentina in 2002.

The results on the final day gave Sale Sharks a third place finish after Bath had lost at home to Leeds Tykes. The first objective had been achieved with the Heineken Cup place earned, but the third place afforded Sale Sharks a chance of becoming Premiership Champions by playing Wasps the following week with the winners playing Leicester Tigers at Twickenham a week later for the big prize.

I watched the game on television at home and Sale Sharks were first out of the starting blocks and were well in the lead by half time. During the first half I saw Robbo score an incredible solo try only for it to be ruled out by the referee as he deemed Sebastien Chabal had been tangling with Matt Dawson on the floor in back play. I defy anyone who watches the footage to agree with the referee and the following day the top journalists like Stephen Jones in the *Sunday Times* gave the officials both barrels. By half time Charlie Hodgson was out of the game after banging heads with Simon Shaw but worse was to come. In the second period Wasps went into the lead and Sale Sharks picked up bad injuries to Steve Hanley (broken leg), Jason White (broken thumb), John Carter (dislocated shoulder), Magnus Lund (bad dead leg) and Andy Titterrell (cut head).

Sale Sharks walked off the field with their heads held high. They had given everything, but the disallowed Jason Robinson try could have proved crucial.

During commentary Stuart Barnes of Sky TV said Jason looked as though he was locked in Pandora's box. I told Robbo and he watched the video before remarking with an inquisitive look, "Who is Pandora?"

Lewsey scored a great try in the first half, and Robbo said he had been wrong footed but paid tribute to the sheer class of Lewsey. I joked to Robbo that he should get a chair lift

BILLY WHIZZ IN THE BEANO
One Billy Whizz gets confused with the other down under
(Reproduced by kind permission of D.C.Thomson & Co Ltd, Dundee)

BACK HOME
Jason scoring against Leeds Tykes, his home town team, March 2004

GENTLEMAN JIM
Sale Sharks Head Coach Jim Mallinder, now in the England set-up

DROP GOAL
Jason scores against Connacht, April 2005

HE'S GOT PACE
Jason on the attack against bourgoin, October 2002

TWICKENHAM WAY
Sale Sharks arrive at HQ for the Powergen Final, April 2004

JASON'S BOOTS
Special Pumas for the Cup
Final, April 2004

TWICKENHAM WAY
Sale Sharks line up at Twickenham

FOILED
Sale Sharks' Cup run ends in defeat, 33-37 at the hands of Newcastle Falcons

DESPAIR
Sale Sharks owner Brian Kennedy consoles Charlie Hodgson

RUCK AND BALL
Jason finds himself at the bottom of the pile in the Wildcard final against Leicester Tigers at Twickenham, May 2004

THE TRY IS GIVEN!
Jason beats Ollie Smith to score as referee Tony Spreadbury awards the try

AUSTIN NEARLY
Jason attempts to stop Leicester's Austin Healey

CAPTAIN ROBINSON
Jason leads Sale at Twickenham

ESCAPED
Jason evades a Tiger tackle in the Wildcard final at Twickenham, May 2004

TRY
Jason about to touch down as Sale lose 27-48 to Leicester Tigers

SALE SHARKS BACK AT TWICKENHAM
The squad lines up before the Wildcard final, May 2004

SEABASS
Sebastien Chabal in support at
Northampton, October 2004

SPIN IT SALE!
Jason releases the ball v
Northampton, January 2005

WONDER TRY
Jason weaves his magic to score
at Newcastle, January 2005

CHARGE
Jason on the attack in the
European Challenge Cup
final at Oxford United's
Kassam Stadium, May 2005

THIN AIR
Jason slips a tackle as
Pau are beaten27-3

FINAL 2005

CHAMPIONS
Jason and Bryan Redpath
hold the cup as Robert
Todd and Andy Titterrell
join in

EUROPEAN UNION
Jason and Philippe Saint Andre hold up the European Challenge Cup at Oxford, May 2005

FAREWELL TRIUMPH
Jos Baxendell and Bryan Redpath share the trophy after playing their last game for Sale Sharks

BACK THREE
The injured Steve Hanley and Mark Cueto get their hands on the trophy

BACKROOM BOYS
Pete Anglesea with legendary kitman Robbie Dickson (left), Swanny and Mark Cueto (right)

THREE LIONS ON THE STEPS
On the day Charlie Hodgson, Jason and Andy Titterrell are called up by the British and Irish Lions,Sharky guards them outside Manchester Town Hall, May 2005

SKY'S THE LIMIT
Sky Sports reporter Graham Simmonds interviews Jason in front of the Town Hall

BESIEGED
Jason in demand at The Stoop, home of Haearlequins

WHO'S NEXT?
Jason signs at Edgeley after the Catania match

WINNING RETURN
Back at Edgeley after the European triumph

LUCKY MASCOTS
Jason meets the mascots at Edgeley

YOUNG FANS
Young Matthew Doyley and his sister are thrilled to meet their hero

TETLEY FAN NIGHT
Dave Swanton, Bryan Redpath, Mark Cueto, Jason White and Jason Robinson answer the questions

SUPPORTERS CLUB
Jason signs more autographs for the supporters

SIGNED SHIRT
Another signed England shirt goes under the hammer

SCARED OF SHARKS! - Jason unnerved by Sharky in the Club Shop

SIGN HERE
More signings in
the Club Shop

FINDING MY FEET
Jason's autobiography in the Club Shop

SWANNY SIGNS
Dave Swanton signing his
autograph for a young fan

MR & MRS
Dave and Carole Swanton
at the Sale Sharks
Awards Dinner June 2005

TRY TIME!
Jason helps Dan Swanton to
celebrate his touch rugby try

MY DEAR OLD SWANNY
Author Dave Swanton

to get him upstairs as he was getting old. He replied, "Not a bad idea Swanny, I use the tread mill in my gym at home to take the dog for a walk you know!"

The players took a few days off after the game to recover from their bumps and bruises although the Lions were away in Cardiff for part of the week. The following Monday I organised the Press Day for the European Challenge Cup Final at the club's training ground in Bramhall. There was a good turn out and the players were on top form as usual. Andrew Sheridan was in big demand though, after his Lions call up. Andrew is a huge man who is quickly becoming a top front row forward in the World game. We slowed the press conference down, because Bryan Redpath had not arrived. Bryan had been in agony with a back injury and had been given two epidural injections in quick time to get him fit for the final. Robbo was aware of why we were slowing down the press day and so were the other players who took their time with their lunch before being interviewed. When Bryan arrived he sprung straight into action and was his usual self, an interviewer's dream.

Bryan was a well-respected player during his long career and both he and Jason had become very close. I feel genuinely sorry for Bryan because he was in his mid-twenties when the game went fully professional and if he had had years on his side he would have been a contender for the best scrum half in the game. He has moved into coaching now as Dean Ryan's assistant at Gloucester and I am sure he will coach the Scotland team in years to come.

After the press Conference I thanked the media for attending and we threw our usual media cloak over the club. John Monie taught me this at Wigan when he told me to get all the press and PR clear as early in the week as possible and tell the media that they could speak to the players *after* the final and not before.

The day after, Mark Cueto received his call-up papers for the Lions and I was so happy for him, as were the rest of the squad. Mark deserved his call-up so much after his consistent week-in-week-out displays as well as his eight tries in eight games for England.

The day before the game I drove down to Oxford with our Press Officer, John Everton. We had a few jobs to do at the Kassam Stadium before relaxing during the evening. When we left the Motorway on the outskirts of Oxford, John took me to lunch at a pub on the banks of the Isis, the local name for the developing River Thames.

I rang Robbo to see if the players had settled in at the hotel. He told me they had a good training session in readiness for the final and had settled in well.

I read the menu from the pub down the mobile phone, as I knew he would be having the usual pre-match meal as a payback for his recent stunts and said I would see him at the game.

I shared a hotel room with John Everton and I must say he snores well - that's the politest way I can put it. I suggested to John that if we travel together to games again we would need to have different floors, let alone separate rooms!

On the morning of the game it was raining heavily and it was thought this would not suit the Sale Sharks way of playing fast open rugby. Before kick off there was a nice gesture from Jason who allowed Bryan Redpath to lead out the team on his final appearance for the club.

Sale Sharks dominated the game throughout and scored four tries. Charlie Hodgson scored two, Mark Cueto and Andy Titterrell one each with Charlie kicking the points.

At the final whistle there were great celebrations on the field and I made my way on to organise the players for interviews with Sky television. Jason lifted the cup with Bryan and Jos Baxendell, the club's longest-serving player. We joked later that it was the biggest birdbath we had ever seen, solid silver too! I was so happy for everyone connected to the club, as we had been pre-season write-offs in some quarters but had finished third and won a cup.

Robbo travelled back with the team and I was asked to load the trophy in my car and take it back to Edgeley Park for the celebrations. Carole helped me carry the huge case containing the cup to the car and we drove non-stop back to Cheshire.

I spoke to Jason on the mobile just before the team returned and said I needed him to sign some items for one of his sponsors. He told me he would do it over the next week or so.

I said, "Robbo, have you not got a diary? You leave with the Lions on Tuesday!"

He told me in confidence that he was not going out with the main tour party, as he wanted to spend some time with Amanda who was expecting in August and that she had not been very well. Sir Clive Woodward made the announcement at the Press Conference on the day before the tour party left which sent some journalists into overdrive as to whether or not he would actually go.

I said, "I know why you are doing this, Robbo. On a tour you are herded through customs and immigration and you don't get time to buy duty frees and you want to get me two hundred cigarettes and a bottle of gin for Carole." I also told him that on the plane he would be 'Billy No Mates' not 'Billy Whizz'.

The mobile phone screening started the following day and when that's in force you get one in ten calls answered otherwise it's 'leave a message time'.

On the Bank Holiday Saturday he rang late in the day and said, "Swanny, are you in your pyjamas?"

"What is this, some type of quiz?" I replied.

"No, the alarm is going off at my old house and needs re-setting," he said.

It was sorted out and I said to him, "If you see a copy of the Autumn Internationals Video from 2002 on your travels will you get me a copy?" I said.

"Why 2002?" He replied.

"I missed that game as it was the last time your alarm went off!" I replied.

Robbo laughed and made an apology. I also told him that Stuart Farmer from SFMS had sent his stats through for this book and that he had played more Rugby Union games than he had first thought. Stuart is the best in his field and the stats are listed game-by-game at the end of this book for you to study.

"No wonder I am clapped out Swanny, I thought I had played about four hundred games not almost five hundred," he said.

"If you look at the stats you will also see that your last try was at Newcastle on the second of January so you are due to get a shed load on the Lions tour!" I said.

"Hey Swanny, remember on the last tour I got ten tries and won the Golden Claw, the trophy given by the *Wales on Sunday* Newspaper," he said.

"I know Robbo, it's still in my filing cabinet at home!" I replied.

"Look after it, Swanny, it's what can I say... different!" he said laughing.

"Robbo, it would frighten a police horse and whenever I get it out of the filing cabinet, Bazil, my dog, barks like mad! Listen pal, if you're neck and neck on tries in the final Test and there are two of you going for the line, offload the ball so you can present the trophy to them!"

It was great to speak to Robbo with him in this mood. He had rested well, Amanda was feeling a lot better and he was ready to board the plane to go and play for the Lions.

He called me at home on the Thursday before he left while I was having a shower. When I rang him back I told him why I had not answered the call and threw in that I had been washing my hair. "With a flannel?" was his quip. Robbo has a thing about hairstyles. He rang once while Carole was giving me a haircut. She answered by telling Robbo I was having my hair done. His reply, laughing of course, was, "I'll hang on!"

We met up at Edgeley Park the day before he left, he was raring to go and looking forward to meeting Inga while he was in New Zealand.

"Keep in touch Robbo, give me a buzz when you land," I said.

"Will do Swanny, and keep me updated with everything that's going on, will you?" he replied.

"Just one thing Robbo, when you run out for the First Test, just think of me sat in bed with a massive bacon sandwich and a mug of tea!" I said.

"Just for that, I'm aiming to be the leading try scorer and win you another trophy to look after!" he said as he left.

LOSING WITH THE LIONS

I had been receiving some calls from the media men who had travelled to New Zealand with the Lions, asking whether Jason would actually be flying over or whether he would be staying at home. I told them all that Robbo was looking forward to the trip. Alex Spink of the *Daily Mirror* wrote a good piece in the paper confirming Robbo was on his way and it stopped the calls, more or less, straight away!

Jason left for New Zealand on Monday 6th June, feeling better in himself after spending some time with Amanda and the children. I spoke to him at the airport while I was driving home from BBC Radio Lancashire and he was looking forward to getting involved with the Lions training sessions and games.

"Hopefully, I will play against Wellington on the 15th and if all goes well I may get selected for the First Test. It won't be easy though, Swanny, there are some very good players in the squad this time, but I can only do my best," he said.

On the following Friday, I had just sat down for my evening meal and he called. I looked at my watch and it was 6 pm, UK time. "What's up pal, can't sleep?" I asked.

"My body clock is all over the place, Swanny, I have been up since 4 am," he said.

"Why not tire yourself out then and get a good night's sleep?" I replied.

"When I arrived on Wednesday afternoon, I did a bike session, watched the game and then yesterday, I did a full weights session, but I am full of energy and want to get playing," he said.

"Watch out New Zealand then, Robbo is raring to go. Fortunately Josh Lewsey has got a head start on you with tries so you will need to pull your finger out to win the top try award again!" I joked.

Robbo laughed, "I have told you I am aiming for that award again."

"Have you found any fast food outlets yet? KFC, Burger King or McDonalds?" I asked.

"Not yet, but there must be some hiding somewhere!" he said.

We talked for about half an hour about various subjects, Philippe's new signings, the poor form that Wigan Rugby League Club were in and the rumours that Kris Radlinski would be the next Rugby League export to Union. Robbo closed by saying that he was going to have his breakfast and start training before going with the squad to the game against the New Zealand Maori.

"Hopefully after a full day, some fresh air and some community work, I will be tired out and this should adjust my body clock," he said.

I sent him a text message later in the evening, with the bad news that Wigan had lost at home to Hull in Super League. He still cares passionately about his old club, although there are very few players remaining at the club from his time there.

The game against the New Zealand Maori finished in defeat. A lot had been made of the big front row the Lions were fielding but the Lions did not play well and were, I thought, on the wrong end of some strange decisions. Andrew Sheridan threw a haymaker at one of the Maoris on the stroke of half time, only to be sin binned. Sherry had been hit first and had retaliated but his attempted punch was in full sight of the referee whereas the blow he had received was a sneaky one. I was just glad he did not connect with his punch, because the opponent would have been visiting Disneyland for a few hours!

The next game for the Lions was against Wellington and Sir Clive was expected to name his big guns for this fixture including Jonny Wilkinson, Gareth Thomas and Robbo.

Robbo rang me to tell me he had been selected and was looking forward to the game. He was originally picked on the right wing to partner Captain Brian O'Driscoll but was moved to the left wing 48 hours before the game and would now partner Gavin Henson. I wished Jason all the best by text message and watched the game with interest. Conditions at the ground were poor in that it rained and there was a strong wind. I spoke to Jason after the game and he said, "I was happy to be playing again, it's almost a month since my last game and it took me a while to shake off my rustiness."

I told him the Sky Panel had not been complimentary about his performance and that they thought he was off the pace and had been for a while.

"Nice to know they're consistent, let's see if we can give them something to talk about in the coming weeks," he said defiantly.

Robbo was still having problems with his lack of sleep and we discussed everything non-Rugby including the flight between the two islands in New Zealand and the wonderful scenery. Finally we organised some tickets for the First Test for a sponsor and said our goodbyes.

The following Sunday Robbo rang to tell me that he would be playing in the First Test and that he was looking forward to the game. We discussed the 70-0 defeat Wigan had suffered the night before at Leeds Rhinos and Robbo was naturally upset that his former team were seemingly in freefall. We agreed though that Ian Millward was a good appointment as Head Coach and that Wigan would recover in time. I also told Robbo that there was a mini heatwave in the

United Kingdom, but added that it was due to finish the day he arrived home in July! Robbo hit back by saying, "Don't forget the sun block on your head then, Swanny!"

The alarm clock went off nice and early on the day of the First Test. I sat in front of the television as millions of others did hoping Sir Clive Woodward's Lions could put one over on the All Blacks in their own backyard. The horror show started within two minutes when Brian O'Driscoll was 'spear tackled' by Umaga and Mealamu. The ball had clearly moved on and I believe the attack on O'Driscoll was cowardly and could also have resulted in a more serious injury than a dislocated shoulder. There have been incidents over the years which have left a sour taste including Colin Meads' sending off in the sixties, JPR Williams having his face raked in a ruck and the South African blood bath in 2002, but the O'Driscoll incident was nothing short of disgraceful. I have the pleasure of working with rugby players and know the risks they take, but 'spear tackles' should not only be outlawed, but the people making these tackles should be banished from the game. Thankfully Rugby League has put its house in order and deals with 'spear tackles' severely. After the game Sir Clive attempted to cite the incident, but it came to nothing, which is sad for the game.

Jason's contribution in the First Test was, as always, scrutinised by the media, and when I rang Robbo, I read some of the written pieces out to him. Robbo likes to hear what writers have to say, good or bad and I have found that if they give him bad press, he will react positively and go out and prove them wrong. One paper, in its review of the First Test, stated that Robbo was "mentally at home with his family, and on this display his body should go too!" Another stated that "thirty is a dangerous age in rugby and Robbo was growing as old as mutton!"

Robbo attended the Manawatu pre-game press conference

and was asked about the mistakes he had made in the First Test. He had responded positively to these claims and he told me later that he thought his kicking game could have been better, but thought the question about him mishandling a pass round his ears was a bit harsh.

I scanned the video that evening and thought the press had not really picked up his try-saving tackle in the 18th minute and a darting run when he made thirty metres was one of the Lions' few attacks in the whole game. Robbo has set high standards and always delivered but unfortunately people now believe he can run the length of the field and sidestep every opponent! He may be good, but not that good! Maybe some are confusing him with the Beano character 'Billy Whizz' too often?

I reminded Robbo of the try he had scored against Newcastle in January, running half the length of the field, weaving his way through the opponents, and told him that people expected him to do this every game.

The problem the Lions had in the First Test was that they could not win their own lineouts and were beaten up in the forwards. Jason, Jonny Wilkinson, Gareth Thomas and Josh Lewsey are World-class players but they need to have the ball in their hands to do something with it.

Carole follows rugby at Sale Sharks and is the first person to admit she does not know the rules or the finer points, but said, "When a red man throws in at the lineout, surely one of the tall red-shirted players should get the ball?" Losing ten of your lineouts in any class of rugby spells defeat. One of the Sale Sharks supporters summed it up perfectly when he said, "If you were appearing on Bullseye hosted by Jim Bowen, you would not like to have Shane Byrne or Steve Thompson throwing for you on that form!"

The Manawatu game was won 109-6 and I got the feeling that maybe the Lions had set their stall out to rescue the tour after the criticism they had received. Manawatu may well have been a part-time outfit but the performance would surely have lifted the whole squad. Robbo got himself on the score sheet on thirty minutes after good work by Chris Cusiter. While it may have been Robbo's first try since January 2nd, the number of tries he has been involved in and his team-mates have scored must not be forgotten.

It was also great to see Mark Cueto get a run-out too. Mark was the form winger in British Rugby Union the previous season and I remember the look on his face when he was finally selected. Charlie Hodgson also did not put a foot wrong and Robbo told me that the boys had been ribbing Charlie because he had been named Vice-Captain for the game.

I spoke to Robbo the day after the game and I congratulated him on his selection for the Second Test. Jason was fully focussed on this game and having known him for many years, I let him do most of the talking as he was in 'Big Game Mode'. Jason was very fortunate to have served his apprenticeship at Wigan where all players were used to the pressures of having to play at the top of their game every week. I did tell him that the newspaper *Wales on Sunday*, had been less than complimentary about his performances on the tour, but he shrugged it off. I did make him laugh though, when I said that Shane Williams' five tries against Manawatu had made him clear leader for the trophy Jason had asked me to look after four years previously!

The next time I spoke to him was breakfast time, New Zealand time, two days before the Second Test. We discussed several topics, but I purposely left the big game alone. Robbo was happy that Mark Nelson had organised a recreation room for the players at the Sale Sharks training ground. Robbo asked me to source a pool table and a dartboard, but when I suggested gaming machines and computer games he knew I was winding him up!

I told Jason that sections of the media had been having a 'pop' at Alastair Campbell but Robbo, ever the diplomat, just said that he was in New Zealand to win a series. He was not interested in all the politics and sniping that had started to take pole position over the matter in hand, which was winning the second and third Test matches.

My own opinion, for what it is worth, is that the Rugby Union press that I deal with are all educated professionals who know what they want to write and will always use their own angle and style, as the Rugby League press do. They are all shrewd operators who would detect instantly if they thought they were being manipulated and, quite simply, it is not worth trying. I have been very fortunate at Wigan, Warrington and Sale Sharks in that the Coaches I have worked for have, more often than not, allowed me to do my job and have rarely stopped the press accessing players. Column inches, television and radio coverage are crucial to Rugby Union and I prefer them to be covering my team as much as possible. Over the years the clear message from the media is that if they don't get the story they will dig for it, and that is dangerous. Players have their preferred journalists and most have a memory like that of an elephant, they never forget! There was a great quote in one of the daily papers that said that a Media Manager should almost be invisible. I believe we stoke the fire and put up the people who matter for interview, not 'hog the limelight'.

The whole of the nation awaited kick-off time at Wellington. The first real attack saw Gareth Thomas score a great try and shortly afterwards a Jonny Wilkinson penalty hit the post. Jason ran in to collect the rebound but sadly nothing came of it. The game showed the All Black domination of the game and they ran out easy winners. I didn't phone Jason after the game but we exchanged text messages and he told me he was okay but disappointed about the defeat.

The following morning I had horrendous toothache and my good friend and dentist, Roger Hughlock, invited me to his surgery for some treatment. As I sat in the car, about to drive home, the phone rang. It was Robbo. We discussed many topics including the game and the media coverage of both the game and the previous week. I told Jason the coverage was kinder to him than the previous week. He replied, "Swanny, when I was sixteen years old the media said I would not make a Rugby player as long as I had a hole in my backside, and I haven't done too badly. I average a try every other game."

I detected that Jason was not really bothered whether he received good press or not. One article that did attract my attention included a quote from former England coach Geoff Cooke who said that Robbo was a shadow of his former self and that he did not understand why Sir Clive had persisted in playing him. It amazes me that people believe that Jason is on the field solely to score tries. His all-round game includes defence and I cannot remember many tackles he missed on the tour. To be able to deliver tries, he needs the ball in his hand, but the supply had dried up on the tour. I remember the first try he scored in his Test debut against Australia in 2001 when the ball flowed across the line and the World Cup Final in 2003 when Dallaglio and Wilkinson sent him in at the corner. On this tour he had so few opportunities to run at defences, he was invariably given the ball when he was standing still and was surrounded by three or more opposition players.

I am a firm believer in asking experienced ex-players their opinion, but when they revert to "the grass was greener in my day, skies were bluer and lineout jumpers could jump ten feet without being lifted" it reminds me of that great Monty

Python sketch.

The game has moved on, it is now a full-time profession and let's be honest, even the most partisan of Rugby fans could not have helped but been impressed by the All Blacks' incredible performance. The British and Irish Lions had hardly any time to prepare for this tour and the All Blacks had excellent preparation. Maybe the 'bringing together', of players from four Nations is past its sell-by date. We spoke for about half an hour and continued the conversation the following day.

When Charlie Hodgson was flattened in the Auckland game, I rang Robbo and asked him to check up how Vice-Captain Charlie was! Half an hour later Robbo sent me a text to say that Charlie was fine and I was able to pass the message around the club.

Robbo rang me on the coach later and said he was going out for a meal. I told him I was having fish and chips for dinner and just to rub it in, I sent him a picture of my lunch by photo-text message. He rang back and said I should watch out when he returned to the UK, as he would pay me back!

The following day, I spoke to Jason on my drive into work and he told me that he had been left out of the team for the Third Test and his place was to be taken by his team-mate, Mark Cueto. Typical of Robbo, he told me that Mark thoroughly deserved his place in the team, as he was the form winger in the Northern Hemisphere. Jason and I discussed the first two Test matches and the lack of ball he'd had. In fact, rather than being in the attacking front line, his defence had been awesome, tackling All Blacks a lot bigger than he was, and on more than one occasion saving certain tries with last-ditch tackles.

We also discussed his knee problem, which had been troubling him on tour. Jason told me that two days after his return to the United Kingdom he was booked in to see a specialist and would probably undergo an operation to cure the problem.

Thinking back and then checking my facts, I found it was the first time he had been left out of a team altogether since the 1994 Challenge Cup Final when then Wigan Coach John Dorahy omitted him from the team. That's not a bad record over eleven years by anyone's standards.

Sir Clive Woodward had nothing to lose with the final fixture and Mark Cueto was being given a chance on the World stage. Mark had enjoyed a phenomenal season with Sale Sharks and England and considering he wasn't a member of the sixty-strong Elite England Squad in 2004 it was a terrific achievement for him.

I closed by telling Jason that the heatwave was due to co-incide with his arrival back home. The Third Test provided to be the 'Blackwash' everybody feared and to be honest I was just glad that there were no injuries, especially to Mark Cueto.

The tour party left Auckland bound for London on Sunday 10th July and the Sale Sharks players, including Robbo, landed at Heathrow in the early hours of Monday morning.

I set off to work early and was in the middle of buying the newspapers in Stockport when the phone rang. It was Robbo. "We're back and shattered with the travelling, but at least the weather forecast for today looks good. I have an appointment with the knee specialist on Wednesday and could be on crutches by the weekend, how's your weekend been, Swanny?"

"Great thanks, went to the JJB on Saturday and saw Wigan beat Warrington and spent most of yesterday on a sun lounger inspecting the inside of my eyelids," I replied.

"Do me favour Swanny, I need full biography and career details of the new players we have signed, can you email them to me today?" he asked. Robbo was preparing for the new season already and was looking forward to leading the team again.

"I will send you those details first thing, speak to you soon pal, good to have you back," I finished.

The day Jason saw the specialist; he rang me on the way home to tell me he needed surgery on both his knee and his ankle. I told him how sorry I was to hear the news but couldn't resist saying, "Are you having a hip replacement too, Robbo?"

"That, Swanny, was as funny as you winning those curling tongues in a raffle," he replied.

On the day of the operation, I spoke to Jeff Ross, one of the Sale Sharks physiotherapists who told me that findings were not as bad as first feared and that Robbo would be back in action sooner than was first thought.

On his way home from hospital Robbo rang and said, "Swanny, I have been rebuilt and have a few more miles on the clock yet!"

I replied, "That's great news Robbo, just one thing though, you are 31 at the end of July, do you now want to be classed as thirty plus VAT on your club biography sheet?"

"See you soon pal, but remember I am going to get you back for the past few weeks. I have been working on my plan for days."

PEOPLE IN THE KNOW

While writing this book I thought I would contact people who have known and played with Jason over the years to get their opinion on 'Billy Whizz'.

Angela Powers of Sky Sports:

"There are two occasions I remember which show two different sides of Jason Robinson. The first was during my early days at Sky Sports when I got a phone call off Swanny, who was then the Media Manager of Wigan Warriors. He had come up with another typically off-the-wall idea for a feature. Swanny told me that he had contacted the Beano about doing a feature on Jason and their comic character 'Billy Whizz'.

"A flight to Glasgow later and we were in possession of some fabulous artwork featuring Jason and 'Billy Whizz' passing the ball to one another in the classic Beano style. Well you can't do a 'Billy Whizz' feature without the man himself, so I approached Jason with my plan, fully expecting him to tell me where to go, at 'Billy Whizz' speed.

"What I wanted, I told him, was for him to sit in the Wigan changing room, reading the *Beano*. I explained that back in the edit suite I would create some graphics in cartoon style... you know, those thought bubbles with some pithy dialogue. Jason - quite a shy man, quiet and unassuming - certainly wouldn't go for it, or so I thought. But he did, and with some gusto. The result? A feature I'm still proud of to this day profiling the humorous side of the man of whom we'd seen much but heard little. And he didn't once complain that we were taking the mick.

"The other feature showed his compassionate side. A few years ago the regional BBC newsroom used to produce the live draw for the Challenge Cup. We'd include little one-minute profiles of a player due to feature in the upcoming round, and on this occasion, we asked Jason if he'd let us accompany him on one of his nights out. No, this wasn't in his hell-raising days; this was at a time when after a Sunday game while the rest of the team were letting their hair down, Jason would join a team of volunteers and head off into the seamier side of Manchester. In the dark, shadowy side of the city, these volunteers would open their vans and serve tea, snacks and give out blankets to the homeless and less fortunate inhabitants of town.

"He didn't make a big song and dance about it; he didn't try to explain in detail what they wanted to achieve. With a shrug he agreed to let us come along and then quietly, in typical Robbo style, he got on with the job. It wasn't a comfortable experience. As someone who'd never seen at first hand the plight of the homeless, I admit I felt nervous and vulnerable. Jason looked totally at ease, saying little as usual, but doing an awful lot. He'd done a lot to highlight the plight of a sector of our society that doesn't get a lot of sympathetic support. And he'd done a lot in person. With his own hands."

Richard Prescott, RFU Director of Communications:

"In New Zealand in 2003, Jason asked me for some information on the new stadium in Wellington. I did all the research including information on the stands, pitch etc and he was very grateful until he asked me if I was sure that the stadium was called the 'Biscuit Tin'. It is of course called the 'Cake Tin'. As biscuits are one of his favourite treats, I'm sure I saw him on a couple of occasions mime putting his hand in a biscuit tin as mickey-take."

Neil Squires of the *Daily Express*:

"Just occasionally, even to a cynical journalist, a job leaps out of the in-tray and whacks you on the nose. The opportunity to tackle Jason Robinson, after taking part in a training session run by him, was one of those clear-the-diary invitations, which relegated staring out of the window and putting the kettle on again to the bottom of the pile. It was a chance to experience in alarming close-up a unique talent at work and it did not disappoint. This is what I wrote afterwards:

'It would have been fairer if there had been a bang and a puff of smoke. One moment a rapidly approaching Jason Robinson is filling my vision, the next he is nowhere to be seen. There is no hole in the ground, no scorched grass, not even a sound as he vanishes. It's like tackling a gust of wind. Robinson's step, Rugby's most watchable magic trick, is even more jaw dropping from the pitch than the stands. The balance and acceleration belong to one of the most highly-tuned sports cars, the change of direction to a zigzag. If Robinson had been born in Wengen rather than West Yorkshire, he would have made some slalom skier.

"I had been given a tip from within the England camp on stopping him ahead of this least exacting of Robinson's World Cup training sessions. Guess which way he is going, head off that way, and if you are right you have a chance. Of course, if you are wrong you miss him by the width of a street. But even when Billy Whizz tells you which foot he is stepping off it is still impossible to lay a hand on him because the swerve which follows takes him so far sideways it would need a lasso to stop him.'

"The article was run alongside a picture of Jason leaving me scrabbling in the dirt in his wake. My colleagues at the *Daily Express*, always supportive, assembled a photomontage of my humiliation, which I was duly presented with at the office Christmas party. It sits above my desk as a reminder never to get too big for my boots – and never be too harsh on anyone who misses a tackle on Robinson.

Paul Cullen, Head Coach of Warrington Wolves who played against Jason:

"We always knew that he posed a threat, but there was nothing we could do about him."

Kingsley Jones, Head Coach of Sale Sharks:

"I was driving to the training ground one morning, when I saw this little guy running away from a Range Rover, at top speed, holding a petrol can. In Alderley Edge, which is a very nice area of Cheshire, you think the worst. I was about to ring the police when I saw it was Jason, who had run out of petrol again!"

Stuart Duffy, Media Manager of the Bradford Bulls: "Many things have been written about Jason Robinson's prowess on the Rugby field, but very little about his persona off it. Jason is an exceptional person with great thought for others. One example that happened a few years ago sums him up superbly.

"It is well known that Jason was 'discovered' by the then Wigan scout Eric Hawley. His hometown club, Leeds had rejected Jason and Eric, who was well aware of Jason's capabilities, took him to Wigan. The rest, they say, is history! A couple of years ago, Eric was working as Chief Scout at Bradford Bulls as well as working as a representative for an educational supply company. When Eric reached retirement age, his employers asked me if I could organise a Bulls player he had signed to come to his retirement party, to present him with his leaving present. I had organised Lee Gilmour, then a Bulls player, and a player Eric had taken to Wigan to attend. I also suggested that perhaps Jason would like to attend.

"The company were delighted with this and asked me to try to arrange something. I rang Swanny at Sale Sharks and he put the idea to Jason. Swanny rang back within five minutes and said that Jason would be delighted to attend and gave me Jason's mobile number to arrange timings. On the day Jason drove all the way to Wakefield, straight from training and presented Eric with one of his Great Britain shirts. Eric was moved to tears to see Jason, who was like a son to him. Jason stayed and chatted to Eric and his colleagues and everyone was impressed with his quiet, unassuming demeanour. That to me sums up Jason completely. He is someone who always puts other people before himself."

Kris Radlinski, his former team-mate, at Wigan Rugby League Club:

"I have been involved in games where people have been amazed at the sheer brilliance of Robbo. He has made some of the best defenders in both codes look quite ordinary when he leaves them grasping at thin air. I would love to play against him and be forced into a one-on-one with him, but think I know what fate would hold in store! I am so proud to call him a friend and have followed his career with Sale Sharks, England and the Lions with interest. Robbo is unique and is the player that other players want to watch and emulate. I would think his name is the first the opponents look for on the team sheet. Robbo is a top bloke with a heart of gold."

Ray French of BBC Grandstand, a former Rugby Union and Rugby League International:

"An enigma! The supreme entertainer in both League and Union. Whether racing down the touchlines and evading the clutches of a despairing tackler before touching down in the corner or collecting a high kick near his own try line and setting off on a jinking, defence-splitting run through the centre of the field, Jason has always captured the attention of the fans.

"And the reason why? Well, few of them, and perhaps Jason himself, ever know what he is going to do next. Will he kick? Will he dart and dash around defenders? Will he race through the tightest of gaps? Or will he indulge himself in a mazy, crazy run across the field leaving opposition and team-mates in his wake? The excitement of watching great players in action is that they do not merely conform to team patterns and styles of play but they produce the unexpected, they try the impossible, and they bring the crowd to their feet by their daring in the face of defeat. Oh yes, and when the final whistle blows they are humble in victory. That's Jason Robinson, the entertainer."

Mark Cueto of Sale Sharks, England and the Lions:

"Jason has given me so much help since I made the first team and is always available to give advice. When he was appointed Captain of Sale Sharks, Steve Hanley and I took it in turns to wind him up. He is the ultimate professional and has taken his role as Captain very seriously. When we were under the cosh at half time at Leicester last season, he entered the dressing room at the same time as Steve and myself and unless my ears deceived me, I heard Robbo swear! He denied this of course, but Steve and I looked at one another and for once we were both speechless."

Chris Irvine of *The Times* who has covered both codes of Rugby:

"Spotting Jason Robinson was like dropping on a second four-leaf clover in the same field. The Rugby League scout Eric Hawley, who also discovered Ellery Hanley, spoke with undisguised passion and glee on the eve of Jason's first Great Britain appearance in 1993. The timing was perfect. Hanley, like Robinson plucked by Hawley from the amateur game in Leeds, bizarrely overlooked by the Leeds club and also ended up at Wigan, had just bowed out of the International scene. Enter Jason at Wembley – two tries in a 17-0 win over New Zealand, blazing a trail of glory past the strapping but hapless figure of Sean Hoppe. 'It's bigger guys every week for a little 'un like me,' Jason had nonchalantly said. A star was born.

It has been a genuine pleasure to deal with Jason in his incredible dozen years at the top. Sure, he had his moments early in his career, but over a cup of tea at Heywood Road or Edgeley Park there are few players so welcoming, or as eager to find out the latest goings-on in his former code. Interviewing him before the 2001 Lions tour, Jason was killing himself laughing. He'd just received his official Lions underwear. Anyone with experience of League tours will know that you're lucky to get an official shirt, never mind embossed boxers. He sat back and chuckled, 'The little scallywag from Leeds, who'd have believed it, eh?'"

Steve Diamond, former Sale Sharks Assistant Coach and now Head Coach at Saracens:

"After the World Cup victory Jason, like the other England players, was in big demand and after a defeat at Wasps there were literally hundreds of fans wanting his autograph. We hatched a plan as to how we could smuggle Jason back to the team coach and I suggested he hid in the wheelie bin we used to carry the kit in! Jason was up for it, but sadly he couldn't quite squeeze inside so he spent an hour signing autographs before we left!"

Keith Mills, who has served Wigan as a player and masseur over forty years:

"The players were once receiving a half-time briefing from John Monie, who said that Jason's fancy footwork was all well and good, but he was moving from side to side on the field rather than making valuable yards in the direction of the opponents' line. Jason said that when he got the ball he did not have any idea where he was going to go. John just left him to carry on in his own unique style."

Mick Hannon, Community Development Manager of Wigan Warriors:

"I remember Jason joining the club as a youngster and

bumping into him one lunchtime at Robin Park in Wigan.

'You will never make it eating that stuff!' I said to the young Wigan winger, who was eating his way through a McDonald's hamburger with fries and swilling it down with a milk shake. 'Give it to me and I'll throw it away.'

"Robbo replied, 'Yeah, and you'll throw them down your throat, that's as far as they'll go!'

"Here I was, at least five stones overweight telling the fastest player in Rugby League how to look after himself. Jason had and still has a very dry sense of humour and added to his flashing smile and quick feet he always eluded me trying to give him a kick up the backside.

"Jason used to visit the local athletics track in Wigan for something to do and he always took an interest especially in the sprinters. Robbo is living proof that junk food in moderation can do you no harm. Just look at his achievements in both codes of Rugby.

"Robbo is a great bloke with a lovely family and it's been a pleasure to be in his company and an honour to call him a friend."

Mike Bradley, formerly of the *Stockport Express* and now with Channel M:

"I've been lucky enough to have met Jason on a number of occasions and always found him willing to give his time which naturally makes my job easier.

"However one of the funniest things I witnessed was the time he inadvertently upset my daughter Cara, at Heywood Road a couple of years ago. I had taken her to watch the Sharks play Bridgend and she spotted Jason sitting in front of us, wrapped in two coats – and wearing Swanny's bobble hat!

"Her eyes lit up when she saw he was eating his way through a large bag of sweets. She gingerly approached him clutching the evening's team sheet and asked him to autograph it for her – which he duly did. However when she returned I could see she was upset.

"'Didn't he give you his autograph?' I asked.

"'Oh yes,' she replied, 'but he didn't give me one of his sweets!'"

Michael 'Braddy' Bradshaw is one of the 'behind the scenes' people in both codes of Rugby. Braddy has worn the suits of the 'Bradford Bull' and 'Flash the Falcon' but his most famous role must be 'Ronnie the Rhino':

"In 2000, Jason's last year in Rugby League, Wigan were playing at Headingley against Leeds on a very warm evening. A streaker ran onto the field and Jason ran after him and made a copybook Rugby tackle. The streaker, worse for drink, got to his feet and squared up to Jason who didn't seem to know what to do next. I intervened and knocked out the streaker while wearing my Ronnie the Rhino suit and then the stewards dragged him away. I think the crowd thought it was all part of the evening's entertainment."

Robbie Dickson is Sale Sharks' popular kit manager:

"One Friday lunchtime after training my nephews Daryl and Chris turned up at Edgeley armed with a camcorder, to ask me if I could persuade any of the players to record a greeting for their dad - my wife Gail's brother - Graham Barlow's 50th birthday. Jason was the first to offer to be filmed, followed by several more players. Graham's face was a picture the following evening when Jason appeared on the big screen at his party with the words 'Happy Birthday, Graham. The lads appreciate your support and hope you have a great evening'." Robbie adds with characteristic enthusiasm: "Jason's an inspiration to the other players and he's a smashin' family man."

THE FUTURE

The last eight years have been a lot of fun. I have two hobbies that I get paid for, working for Sale Sharks and working on BBC Radio Lancashire.

Jason has at least two seasons left at Sale Sharks. I am sure we will build up more lasting memories before he hangs up his boots for the last time.

He will, no doubt, continue to make the headlines and excite Rugby crowds with his unique talents.

This book was written to share my memories of a great man, good friend and highly witty individual. When my mobile phone rings and displays 'Private Number' I am always on guard in case he uses his voice disguise skills.

The road I have travelled at Sale Sharks has been great fun from day one and the progress the club has made under Brian Kennedy and Ian Blackhurst is nothing short of phenomenal.

Who knows what Jason will do when he retires from playing? I cannot see him coaching but I have suggested a career in radio or television. I am sure he will be a big success in whatever road he chooses after he finishes playing but until that day arrives there are more fun and games ahead.

The book was in the process of being printed when Jason rang me while I was on holiday in Madeira. He told me that he was retiring from International Rugby with immediate effect. He was upbeat and said that he was looking forward to spending more time with his family. The travelling up and down the M1 and around the M25 together with the time away from home had, I believe, taken its toll, and he 'wanted out' of this way of life.

We spoke about the great times he's had playing for England, and the conversation ended with Jason saying, "Turn off your mobile phone now, Swanny and enjoy the rest of your break - but don't forget to bring me some Madeira cake back with you."

Hope you enjoyed the book,

Best Wishes,

Swanny

DID YOU KNOW?

★   Jason wears size eight boots.

★   His boots are specially made by Puma and Jason regularly visits the workshop in Leeds where the leather is prepared.

★   Jason is frightened of heights.

★   Jason was a ball boy at Headingley, Leeds, as a youngster and he would try to get the ball to pass back to his hero Gary Schofield.

★   Jason started his rugby career as a scrum half.

★   Jason enjoys the music of the Drifters, Otis Redding, Lionel Richie and also enjoys Tamla Motown.

★   His first memories of music were hand me down Spandau Ballet albums from his brother.

★   Jason never reads newspapers and rarely watches television.

★   He was the first player in Rugby League to win both the Harry Sunderland and Lance Todd Man of the Match Trophies.

★   He is a member of the Beano Fan Club and his membership number is 2, which was his shirt number at Wigan for many years. Other members include Alan Shearer, Michael Owen, Chris Evans, Tony Blair and Princes William and Harry.

★   He had to wait until his final season at Wigan to be awarded the squad number five, by Dean Bell. Jason had always wanted this number but for many seasons it was worn by Martin Offiah.

★   Both Jason and his son Cameron own quad bikes and race them around the garden.

★   Jason does not enjoy swimming and once appeared at a Wigan Warriors water session wearing goggles and sitting on a blow up bed.

★   Sang Saturday Night At The Movies on the bus after his England Rugby Union debut.

★   He passed his driving test at the second attempt.

★   His first car was an Escort Eclipse.

* ★   Jason currently drives a Range Rover.
* ★   His favourite subject at school was PE.
* ★   He would have become an apprentice bricklayer if Wigan had not offered him a professional contract.
* ★   While Jason does not follow a football team he does admit to looking for Leeds United results.
* ★   He played in the 1995 Rugby League Challenge Cup Final with a broken bone in his foot. He was given a pain-killing injection before the game and went on to win Man of the Match, having scored two tries.
* ★   Jason is able to 'moonwalk'.
* ★   Jason has played rugby in England, Scotland, Wales, Ireland, France, Italy, Australia and New Zealand.
* ★   Played at number 13 (8 in Rugby Union) for Wigan in their 78-0 win over Swinton at Gigg Lane Bury in September 1992. Shaun Edwards scored a record ten tries for Wigan in that game.
* ★   Jason played in every position in the back line for Wigan.
* ★   Jason is still unsure about many of the rules in Rugby Union.
* ★   Was sinbinned once in Rugby League and has been yellow carded twice in Rugby Union since his switch in 2000.
* ★   Still jointly holds the Super League record of five tries in a game (for Wigan v Leeds 1996).
* ★   Played for Wigan against Brisbane Broncos at the ANZ Stadium in 1994 in the World Club Championship and scored a try in the Wigan win.
* ★   Spent four months with Bath in the winter of 1996 and represented them in the European Cup as well as the Premiership.
* ★   Was a member of the Dream Team in Rugby League every season from 1996-2000.
* ★   Scored 184 tries in Rugby League in 302 games.

STATISTICS

RUGBY UNION - Compiled by Stuart Farmer Media Services Limited

RUGBY LEAGUE - Compiled by Mike Latham

GAME	DATE	OPPONENTS	VENUE	COMPETITION	RESULT	SHIRT	NOTES	SCORING
	2001	**BRITISH & IRISH LIONS**						
1	Tue 12 Jun 01	Queensland President's XV	Townsville		W 83-6	11		5 Tries
2	Sat 16 Jun 01	Queensland Reds	Ballymore, Brisbane		W 42-8	17	rep	
3	Tue 19 Jun 01	Australia A	Gosford		L 25-28	11		Try
4	Sat 23 Jun 01	NSW Waratahs	Sydney FS		W 41-24	11		2 Tries
5	Sat 30 Jun 01	Australia	Wooloongabba, Brisbane	1st Test	W 29-13	11		Try
6	Sat 7 Jul 01	Australia	Telstra Dome, Melbourne	2nd Test	L 14-35	11		
7	Sat 14 Jul 01	Australia	Telstra Stadium, Sydney	3rd Test	L 23-29	11		Try
	2005	**BRITISH & IRISH LIONS**						
8	15 Jun 05	Wellington	Westpac Std, Wellington		W 23-6	11		
9	Sat 25 Jun 05	New Zealand	Jade Stadium, Christchurch	1st Test	L 3-21	15	replaced	
10	Tue 28 Jun 05	Manawatu	Palmerston North		W 109-6	14	replaced	Try
11	Sat 2 Jul 05	New Zealand	Westpac Std, Wellington	2nd Test	L 18-48	14		
	2000-2001	**ENGLAND**						
1	Sat 17 Feb 01	Italy	Twickenham	Six Nations	W 80-23	22	rep	
2	Sat 3 Mar 01	Scotland	Twickenham	Six Nations	W 43-3	22	rep	
3	Sat 7 Apr 01	France	Twickenham	Six Nations	W 48-19	22	rep	
	2001-2002	**ENGLAND**						
4	Sat 20 Oct 01	Ireland	Lansdowne Road	Six Nations	L 14-20	11		
5	Sat 10 Nov 01	Australia	Twickenham	Cook Cup	W 21-15	15		
6	Sat 17 Nov 01	Romania	Twickenham		W 134-0	15		4 Tries
7	Sat 24 Nov 01	South Africa	Twickenham		W 29-9	15		

GAME	DATE	OPPONENTS	VENUE	COMPETITION	RESULT	SHIRT	NOTES	SCORING
8	Sat 2 Feb 02	Scotland	Murrayfield	Six Nations	W 29-3	15		2 Tries
9	Sat 16 Feb 02	Ireland	Twickenham	Six Nations	W 45-11	15		
10	Sat 2 Mar 02	France	Stade de France	Six Nations	L 15-20	15		Try
11	Sun 7 Apr 02	Italy	Stadio Flaminio	Six Nations	W 45-9	15		Try
	2002-2003	**ENGLAND**						
12	Sat 9 Nov 02	New Zealand	Twickenham		W 31-28	15		
13	Sat 16 Nov 02	Australia	Twickenham	Cook Cup	W 32-31	15		
14	Sat 23 Nov 02	South Africa	Twickenham		W 53-3	15		
15	Sat 15 Feb 03	France	Twickenham	Six Nations	W 25-17	15		Try
16	Sat 22 Feb 03	Wales	Millennium Stadium	Six Nations	W 26-9	15	replaced	
17	Sat 22 Mar 03	Scotland	Twickenham	Six Nations	W 40-9	14	Yellow card	2 Tries
18	Sun 30 Mar 03	Ireland	Lansdowne Road	Six Nations	W 42-6	14		
19	Sat 14 Jun 03	New Zealand	Westpac Stadium, Wellington		W 15-13	14		
20	Sat 21 Jun 03	Australia	Telstra Dome, Melbourne	Cook Cup	W 25-14	14		
	2003-2004	**ENGLAND**						
21	Sat 6 Sep 03	France	Twickenham		W 45-14	15		Try
22	Sun 12 Oct 03	Georgia	Subiaco Oval, Perth	World Cup	W 84-6	14		Try
23	Sat 18 Oct 03	South Africa	Subiaco Oval, Perth	World Cup	W 25-6	14		
24	Sun 26 Oct 03	Samoa	Telstra Dome, Melbourne	World Cup	W 35-22	15		
25	Sun 2 Nov 03	Uruguay	Suncorp Stadium, Brisbane	World Cup	W 111-13	22	rep	2 Tries
26	Sun 9 Nov 03	Wales	Suncorp Stadium, Brisbane	World Cup QF	W 28-17	15		
27	Sun 16 Nov 03	France	Telstra Stadium, Sydney	World Cup SF	W 24-7	14		
28	Sat 22 Nov 03	Australia	Telstra Stadium, Sydney	World Cup Final	W 20-17	14		Try
29	Sun 15 Feb 04	Italy	Stadio Flaminio	Six Nations	W 50-9	12	replaced	3 Tries

GAME	DATE	OPPONENTS	VENUE	COMPETITION	RESULT	SHIRT	NOTES	SCORING
30	Sat 21 Feb 04	Scotland	Murrayfield	Six Nations	W 35-13	12		
31	Sat 6 Mar 04	Ireland	Twickenham	Six Nations	L 13-19	12		
32	Sat 20 Mar 04	Wales	Twickenham	Six Nations	W 31-21	15		
33	Sat 27 Mar 04	France	Stade de France	Six Nations	L 21-24	15		
	2004-2005	**ENGLAND**					capt.	
34	Sat 13 Nov 04	Canada	Twickenham	Six Nations	W 70-0	15	Replaced	3 Tries
35	Sat 20 Nov 04	South Africa	Twickenham	Six Nations	W 32-16	15	capt	
36	Sat 27 Nov 04	Australia	Twickenham	Cook Cup	L 19-21	15	capt	
37	Sat 5 Feb 05	Wales	Millennium Stadium	Six Nations	L 9-11	15	capt	
38	Sun 13 Feb 05	France	Twickenham	Six Nations	L 17-18	15	capt	
39	Sun 27 Feb 05	Ireland	Lansdowne Road	Six Nations	L 13-19	15	capt	
	2001-2002	**ENGLAND A**						
1	Fri 2 Feb 01	Wales A	Wrexham		D 19-19 11			
	2003-2004	**ENGLAND XV**						
1	Sat 20 Dec 03	NZ Barbarians	Twickenham		W 42-17 15			

CLUB RUGBY UNION

GAME	DATE	OPPONENTS	VENUE	COMPETITION	RESULT	SHIRT	NOTES	SCORING
	1996-1997	**BATH**						
1	Sat 14 Sep 96	London Wasps	Recreation Ground	Division One	L 36-40	11		Try
2	Sat 21 Sep 96	Gloucester	Kingsholm	Division One	W 45-29	14		Try
3	Sat 5 Oct 96	London Irish	The Avenue	Division One	W 56-31	14		2 Tries
4	Sat 12 Oct 96	Edinburgh Rugby	Recreation Ground	European Cup	W 55-26	14		Try
5	Sat 19 Oct 96	Pontypridd	Sardis Road	European Cup	L 6-19	11		
6	Sat 26 Oct 96	Dax	Recreation Ground	European Cup	W 25-16	14		
7	Tue 29 Oct 96	Bristol Shoguns	Recreation Ground	Division One	W 76-7	15		
8	Sat 2 Nov 96	Benetton Treviso	Stadio di Monigo	European Cup	W 50-27	14		
9	Sat 16 Nov 96	Cardiff	Arms Park	European Cup SF	L 19-22	15		
10	Sat 7 Dec 96	NEC Harlequins	Recreation Ground	Division One	W 35-20	14		
11	Sat 21 Dec 96	London Irish	Recreation Ground	Cup 5th round	W 33-0	14		
12	Sat 4 Jan 97	Saracens	Recreation Ground	Division One	W 35-33	11		
13	Sat 11 Jan 97	NEC Harlequins	The Stoop	Division One	L 6-22	11		
	2000-2001	**SALE SHARKS**						
1	Sun 5 Nov 00	Coventry	Heywood Road	Cup 4th round	W 37-19	11		Try
2	Sun 12 Nov 00	Rotherham Titans	Heywood Road	Cup 5th round	W 20-12	11		
3	Sun 19 Nov 00	Bath Rugby	Recreation Ground	Premiership	L 32-34	11		
4	Sun 26 Nov 00	London Wasps	Loftus Road	Premiership	L 24-33	11		
5	Sat 2 Dec 00	NEC Harlequins	Heywood Road	Premiership	W 35-10	11		2 Tries
6	Sun 10 Dec 00	Waterloo Drummers	Heywood Road	Cup QF	W 59-12	11		Try
7	Sat 16 Dec 00	Rotherham Titans	Heywood Road	Premiership	W 45-12	11		
8	Sat 23 Dec 00	Bristol Shoguns	Heywood Road	Premiership	L 25-26	11		

GAME	DATE	OPPONENTS	VENUE	COMPETITION	RESULT	SHIRT	NOTES	SCORING
9	Sat 6 Jan 01	Newcastle Falcons	Kingston Park	Cup SF	L 25-37	11		
10	Sun 11 Feb 01	Saracens	Vicarage Road	Premiership	L 30-44	11		
11	Sat 24 Feb 01	Northampton Saints	Franklin's Gardens	Premiership	L 26-32	15		Try
12	Tue 6 Mar 01	Leicester Tigers	Welford Road	Premiership	L 12-24	15		
13	Sun 11 Mar 01	Newcastle Falcons	Kingston Park	Premiership	L 24-48	15		
14	Sat 17 Mar 01	Gloucester	Heywood Road	Premiership	L 16-24	15		Try
15	Sat 24 Mar 01	Rotherham Titans	Clifton Lane	Premiership	W 39-13	15		Try
16	Sat 31 Mar 01	NEC Harlequins	The Stoop	Premiership	L 10-36	15		
17	Tue 10 Apr 01	London Irish	Heywood Road	Premiership	W 43-18	15		Try
18	Sat 14 Apr 01	London Wasps	Heywood Road	Premiership	L 29-59	15		Try
					Total	18		9 tries
	2001-2002							
19	Sun 2 Sep 01	**SALE SHARKS** Bristol Shoguns	Memorial Stadium	Premiership	W 35-25	15		
20	Sat 8 Sep 01	Newcastle Falcons	Heywood Road	Premiership	W 37-11	15		Try
21	Sun 16 Sep 01	London Wasps	Loftus Road	Premiership	W 40-21	15		Try
22	Sat 22 Sep 01	Gloucester	Heywood Road	Premiership	L 21-44	15		Try
23	Sat 13 Oct 01	Bath Rugby	Recreation Ground	Premiership	L 17-20	11		
24	Sat 1 Dec 01	NEC Harlequins	The Stoop	Premiership	W 23-16	15		Try
25	Sat 8 Dec 01	London Irish	Heywood Road	Premiership	D 19-19	15		
26	Sat 15 Dec 01	NEC Harlequins	Heywood Road	Cup 6th round	L 25-32	15		
27	Thu 27 Dec 01	Leicester Tigers	Welford Road	Premiership	L 10-33	15		Try
28	Fri 25 Jan 02	Bristol Shoguns	Heywood Road	Euro Shield QF	W 25-20	13		
29	Sat 9 Feb 02	Northampton Saints	Franklin's Gardens	Premiership	W 20-10	13		Try
30	Sat 23 Feb 02	Bath Rugby	Heywood Road	Premiership	W 20-14	15		

GAME	DATE	OPPONENTS	VENUE	COMPETITION	RESULT	SHIRT	NOTES	SCORING
31	Sat 9 Mar 02	Gloucester	Kingsholm	Premiership	L 14-42	15		
32	Sat 16 Mar 02	London Wasps	Heywood Road	Premiership	W 27-22	15	Replaced	
33	Sat 13 Apr 02	Bristol Shoguns	Heywood Road	Premiership	W 53-47	15		Try
34	Fri 19 Apr 02	Saracens	Heywood Road	Premiership	W 23-3	15		
35	Sun 28 Apr 02	Gloucester	Franklin's Gardens	Euro Shield SF	W 28-27	15		
36	Sun 5 May 02	London Irish	Madejski Stadium	Premiership	W 36-32	15		Try
37	Wed 8 May 02	Leeds Tykes	Heywood Road	Premiership	W 35-20	15		
38	Sun 12 May 02	NEC Harlequins	Heywood Road	Premiership	W 40-11	15		
39	Sun 19 May 02	London Wasps	Heywood Road	Premiership	W 43-27	17	Rep	
40	Sun 26 May 02	Pontypridd	Kassam Stadium, Oxford	Euro Shield Final	W 25-22	15		
41	Sun 2 Jun 02	Gloucester	Heywood Road	Championship SF	L 11-33	15		
							22+1	9 tries
	2002-2003	**SALE SHARKS**						
42	Fri 30 Aug 02	Northampton Saints	Heywood Road	Premiership	W 24-21	15		
43	Sat 7 Sep 02	Gloucester	Kingsholm	Premiership	L 8-44	15		
44	Fri 13 Sep 02	Leicester Tigers	Heywood Road	Premiership	W 29-16	15		
45	Fri 20 Sep 02	Leeds Tykes	Headingley	Premiership	D 29-29	15		
46	Fri 27 Sep 02	NEC Harlequins	Heywood Road	Premiership	W 20-16	15		
47	Sat 5 Oct 02	London Irish	Heywood Road	Premiership	W 36-14	15		
							Replaced	
48	Fri 11 Oct 02	Bourgoin-Jallieu	Heywood Road	European Cup	L 18-24	15	Yellow	Try
49	Sun 27 Oct 02	Newcastle Falcons	Kingston Park	Premiership	L 20-31	15		
50	Fri 1 Nov 02	Bristol Shoguns	Heywood Road	Premiership	W 28-14	13		Try
51	Fri 29 Nov 02	Bath Rugby	Heywood Road	Premiership	W 36-18	22	Rep	
52	Fri 6 Dec 02	Llanelli	Heywood Road	European Cup	L 19-30	16	rep	
53	Fri 13 Dec 02	Llanelli	Stradey Park	European Cup	L 12-17	15	capt	

GAME	DATE	OPPONENTS	VENUE	COMPETITION	RESULT	SHIRT	NOTES	SCORING
54	Sun 22 Dec 02	Saracens	Vicarage Road	Cup 6th round	L 20-26	15		
55	Sun 29 Dec 02	Bristol Shoguns	Memorial Stadium	Premiership	L 6-18	15		
56	Fri 3 Jan 03	Newcastle Falcons	Heywood Road	Premiership	W 38-3	15		Try
57	Fri 10 Jan 03	Glasgow Rugby	Heywood Road	European Cup	W 45-3	15		Try
58	Sun 2 Feb 03	London Irish	Madejski Stadium	Premiership	W 23-11	15		
59	Sat 8 Feb 03	NEC Harlequins	The Stoop	Premiership	W 45-0	15	replaced	
60	Sat 15 Mar 03	Leeds Tykes	Heywood Road	Premiership	W 32-20	15		2 Tries
61	Sun 6 Apr 03	Leicester Tigers	Welford Road	Premiership	L 20-33	15		
62	Fri 18 Apr 03	Gloucester	Heywood Road	Premiership	D 30-30	15		Try
63	Sat 26 Apr 03	Northampton Saints	Franklin's Gardens	Premiership	L 17-27	15		
64	Sat 3 May 03	London Wasps	Heywood Road	Premiership	L 9-16	13		
65	Sat 10 May 03	Saracens	Vicarage Road	Premiership	L 19-34	15		2 Tries
							22+2	9 tries
	2003-2004							
66	Sat 6 Dec 03	**SALE SHARKS** Cardiff Blues	Edgeley Park	European Cup	W 26-24	11		
67	Sat 13 Dec 03	Biarritz Olympique	P d Sports Aguilera	European Cup	L 3-31	15	capt	
68	Sat 27 Dec 03	Rotherham Titans	Edgeley Park	Premiership	W 35-7	12		Try
69	Sun 4 Jan 04	London Wasps	Causeway Stadium	Premiership	L 10-26	12		
70	Fri 9 Jan 04	Leinster	Lansdowne Road	European Cup	W 23-22	15		
71	Sun 18 Jan 04	Leinster	Edgeley Park	European Cup	L 16-23	15		
72	Sun 25 Jan 04	Biarritz Olympique	Edgeley Park	European Cup	L 0-15	15		
73	Sat 31 Jan 04	Cardiff Blues	Arms Park	European Cup	L 7-22	21	rep	
74	Fri 6 Feb 04	Leicester Tigers	Edgeley Park	Premiership	D 3-3	15	Capt	
75	Fri 27 Feb 04	Saracens	Edgeley Park	Cup QF	W 26-3	15	Replaced	

GAME	DATE	OPPONENTS	VENUE	COMPETITION	RESULT	SHIRT	NOTES	SCORING
76	Sat 13 Mar 04	Leeds Tykes	Edgeley Park	Cup SF	W 33-20	15		Try
77	Sat 3 Apr 04	Bath Rugby	Recreation Ground	Premiership	L 12-16	15		
78	Sat 17 Apr 04	Newcastle Falcons	Twickenham	Cup Final	L 33-37	15		
79	Fri 23 Apr 04	Newcastle Falcons	Edgeley Park	Premiership	W 41-16	15		
80	Sun 2 May 04	Saracens	Vicarage Road	Premiership	L 23-39	15		
81	Sat 8 May 04	Leeds Tykes	Headingley	Premiership	W 31-20	15		3 Tries
82	Sat 15 May 04	Gloucester	Kingsholm	Wildcard SF	L 35-44	15	Capt	Try
83	Sat 29 May 04	Leicester Tigers	Twickenham	Wildcard Final	L 27-48	15	17+1	6 tries
	2004-2005							
84	Sun 5 Sep 04	Leicester Tigers	Edgeley Park	Premiership	W 26-19	15	Capt	Try
85	Sat 11 Sep 04	London Wasps	Causeway Stadium	Premiership	W 33-30	15	Capt	Drop
86	Fri 17 Sep 04	Saracens	Edgeley Park	Premiership	W 25-15	15	Capt	
87	Fri 24 Sep 04	Worcester Warriors	Edgeley Park	Premiership	W 57-3	15	Capt	Try
88	Sun 3 Oct 04	Leeds Tykes	Headingley	Premiership	W 14-11	15	Capt	
89	Fri 8 Oct 04	London Irish	Edgeley Park	Premiership	L 16-17	15	Capt	
90	Sat 16 Oct 04	Northampton Saints	Franklin's Gardens	Premiership	W 23-6	15	Capt	
91	Fri 5 Nov 04	Newcastle Falcons	Edgeley Park	Premiership	W 39-25	15	Capt	
92	Sat 4 Dec 04	Narbonne	Parc des Sports	Euro Challenge 2nd	W 33-15	15	Capt Capt.	Drop
93	Fri 10 Dec 04	Narbonne	Edgeley Park	Euro Challenge 2nd	W 25-10	15	Replaced	
94	Mon 27 Dec 04	Bath Rugby	Edgeley Park	Premiership	W 19-10	15	Capt	
95	Sun 2 Jan 05	Newcastle Falcons	Kingston Park	Premiership	L 29-30	15	Capt	2 Tries
96	Fri 7 Jan 05	Agen	Edgeley Park	Euro Challenge QF	W 34-18	15	Capt	

GAME	DATE	OPPONENTS	VENUE	COMPETITION	RESULT	SHIRT	NOTES	SCORING
97	Fri 21 Jan 05	Bath Rugby	Edgeley Park	Cup QF	L 23-24	15	Capt. Replaced	
98	Sat 29 Jan 05	Northampton Saints	Edgeley Park	Premiership	W 37-24	15	Capt	
99	Fri 18 Feb 05	Leeds Tykes	Edgeley Park	Premiership	W 19-10	15	Capt	
100	Sat 2 Apr 05	Connacht	Sportsground	Euro Challenge SF	W 25-18	15	Capt	
101	Sat 9 Apr 05	Leicester Tigers	Welford Road	Premiership	L 15-45	15	Capt	
102	Fri 15 Apr 05	Gloucester	Edgeley Park	Premiership	W 35-17	15	Capt	
103	Sun 24 Apr 05	Connacht	Edgeley Park	Euro Challenge SF	W 59-9	15	Capt	Drop
104	Sat 30 Apr 05	NEC Harlequins	The Stoop	Premiership	W 23-22	13	Capt	
105	Sat 7 May 05	London Wasps	Causeway Stadium	Premiership SF	L 22-43	15	Capt	
106	Sat 21 May 05	Pau	Kassam Stadium, Oxford	Euro Challenge Final	W 27-3	15	Capt	4 t + 3dg
							23+1	

SALE SHARKS CAREER SUMMARY

SALE SHARKS	STARTS	REPS	TRIES	DROPS	POINTS
2000-2001	18	-	9	-	45
2001-2002	22	1	9	-	45
2002-2003	22	2	9	-	45
2003-2004	17	1	6	-	30
2004-2005	23	-	4	3	29
TOTALS	**102**	**4**	**37**	**3**	**194**

RUGBY UNION CAREER SUMMARY

TEAM	STARTS	REPS	TRIES	DROPS	POINTS
BATH	13	-	5	-	25
SALE	102	4	37	3	194
ENGLAND A	1	-	-	-	-
ENGLAND XV	1	-	-	-	-
ENGLAND	35	4	22	-	110
LIONS	10	1	11	-	55
TOTALS	**162**	**9**	**75**	**3**	**384**

MAJOR HONOURS - ENGLAND:
WORLD CUP WINNERS: 2003
SIX NATIONS WINNERS: 2001, 2003 (GRAND SLAM)

MAJOR HONOURS - SALE SHARKS:
EUROPEAN CHALLENGE CUP WINNERS: 2001-02, 2004-05
POWERGEN CUP FINALISTS 2003-04
PREMIERSHIP RUNNERS-UP: 2001-02

JASON ROBINSON IN RUGBY LEAGUE

COMPILED BY MIKE LATHAM

CLUB RUGBY LEAGUE

WIGAN	STARTS	REPS	TRIES	DROPS	POINTS
1992-93	35	6	13	0	52
1993-94	29	1	11	0	44
1994-95	35	0	23	0	92
1995-96	24	0	18	0	72
1996	25	0	26	1	105
1997	31	0	20	0	80
1998	29	1	17	0	68
1999	31	0	20	0	80
2000	34	0	23	0	92
TOTALS	**273**	**8**	**171**	**1**	**685**

INTERNATIONAL RUGBY LEAGUE

INTERNATIONAL	STARTS	REPS	TRIES	DROPS	POINTS
GB U-21s					
1992-93	1	0	0	0	0
1993-94	1	0	2	0	8
1994-95	3	0	0	0	0
ENGLAND					
1994-95	1	0	1	0	4
1995-96	4	0	3	0	12
1996	2	0	1	0	4
GB					
1997	3	0	3	0	12
1998	3	0	3	0	12
1999	2	0	0	0	0
GB Tour					
1999	1	0	0	0	0
TOTALS	**21**	**0**	**13**	**0**	**52**

Also played twice for GB Academy in 1992 v France (non first-class games)

RUGBY LEAGUE CAREER SUMMARY

Wigan	273	8	171	1	685
International	21	0	13	0	52
TOTALS	294	8	184	1	737

MAJOR HONOURS:

Championship winners:
1992-93, 1993-94, 1994-95, 1995-96

Super League champions:
1998; runners up 2000

Challenge Cup winners:
1993, 1995; runners up: 1998

Regal Trophy winners:
1992-93, 1994-95, 1995-96; runners up 1993-94

Premiership Trophy winners:
1993-94, 1994-95, 1996, 1997; runners up: 1992-93

Lancashire Cup winners 1992-93
Charity Shield winners 1995-96; runners up: 1992-93

World Club Challenge winners:
1993-94; runners up: 1992-93

Won Harry Sunderland Trophy as outstanding player in 1998 Super League Grand Final

INDEX

Oakes, John 32
Oakes, Phil 36
O'Connor, Terry 14
O'Driscoll, Brian 154, 155
O'Gara, Ronan 51
Osbourne, Ozzy 123

Paul, Henry 4, 17, 20
Penny, Lee 2, 17, 30
Perelini, Apollo 34, 37, 38, 41, 52, 53, 54, 55, 57, 65, 66, 71, 74, 83, 85
Perry, Matt 58
Peters, Willie 25, 26, 37
Pickavance, Ian 2
Pinkerton, Stuart 50, 54, 107
Pinkney, Nick 15
Powers, Angela 18, 36, 163
Prescott, Richard 99, 100, 104, 131, 132, 142, 164

Radlinski, Kris 15, 19, 27, 37, 153, 167
Redpath, Bryan 40, 76, 88, 89, 108, 120, 124, 125, 133, 144, 147, 148
Renouf, Steve 32
Richards, Dean 116
Richie, Lionel 119
Riddoch, Ian 26, 28, 33
Robinson, Amanda 14, 15, 19, 39, 40, 49, 52, 59, 78, 94, 102, 115, 118, 119, 122, 123, 149, 150, 152
Robinson, Andy 131, 132
Robinson, Cameron 14, 19, 52, 59, 90
Robinson, Jemima 59
Robinson, Joseph 78
Robinson, Lisa 62, 138
Roddam, Johnny 126
Rogers, David 58
Ross, Glen 45
Ross, Jeff 162

Royle, Jim 123
Ryan, Dean 147

Sailor, Wendell 7
Saint Andre, Philippe 55, 56, 77, 110, 111, 114, 119, 120, 121, 126, 127, 128, 133, 134, 137, 142, 143, 144, 153
Sanderson, Alex 120
Schofield, Dean 121
Schofield, Gary 23
Shaw, Martin 69
Shaw, Simon 146
Shelford, Kelly 4
Sheridan, Andrew 128, 130, 133, 147, 153
Sinclair, Michelle 65
Smith, John 4, 5, 6
Smith, Paul 122
Smith, Quentin 57, 107
Smith, Russell 18
Smith, Steve 36, 47, 84
Smith, Trevor 92
Smyth, Rob 9
Spink, Alex 152
Squires, Neil 73, 165
Stafford, Ian 139
Stephens, Paul 73
Stephenson, Mike 141
Sudworth, Mike 8
Swann, Willie 4
Swanton, Carole 1, 5, 6, 15, 19, 22, 28, 32, 33, 35, 37, 41, 42, 50, 51, 58, 68, 78, 85, 99, 103, 104, 109, 127, 130, 132, 137, 149, 151, 156
Swanton, Dan 6, 53, 54, 57, 58, 61, 62, 63, 64, 67, 68, 69, 74, 75, 85, 90, 105

Tait, Matthew 134
Thomas, Gareth 154, 156, 158

INDEX